12 STEPS TO SPIRITUAL FREEDOM

Understanding the

CHRISTIAN ROOTS
of TWELVE STEP
PROGRAMS

Joanna Thyer

LOYOLA PRESS.
A JESUIT MINISTRY
Chicago

LOYOLA PRESS.
A JESUIT MINISTRY

3441 N. Ashland Avenue
Chicago, Illinois 60657
(800) 621-1008
www.loyolapress.com

Cover art credit: ©iStockphoto.com/tomograf.

Back cover author photo credit: Luke Stambouliah.

ISBN-13: 978-0-8294-4052-2
ISBN-10: 0-8294-4052-6
Library of Congress Control Number: 2013952545

Printed in the United States of America.

13 14 15 16 17 18 Versa 10 9 8 7 6 5 4 3 2 1

To the "Father of My Soul,"
Brian Stoney

Contents

My Story: In the Desert

I will now persuade her, and bring her into the wilderness, and speak tenderly to her.

—Hosea 2:14

It was in the early 1980s that I first encountered my own kind of biblical desert, both literally and figuratively. In July 1983 I had joined a twelve-step recovery program, a move that brought about a huge shift away from the way I had been living. A couple of years later I was staying in a hotel on a stopover in Amman, Jordan, on my way to making the obligatory pilgrimage of youth: the whirlwind three-week European bus tour, to see how the other half lived.

It was nighttime, and as I sat on my bed and looked out toward the desert, something happened. I felt a spiritual pull I could not explain, a sense of awe and mystery I had not experienced before. I had little belief in God then, except for a no-frills belief in a higher power. Yet I felt God calling me in the desert that night. In a sense, that was the beginning of my faith journey in earnest, yet at that stage it was only a dim bell that I only heard ever so faintly and did not understand—a small but significant esoteric experience, similar to the epiphany of the artist in James Joyce's classic novel *A Portrait of the Artist as a Young Man*, in which I was taken into another dimension, ever so briefly, but profoundly.

Close to a decade later, in the 1990s, my faith journey began in a different way after I suffered a nervous breakdown following the loss of a potential baby. I had become isolated during that period, distant from God, distant from others, chronically depressed, and completely disconnected from myself. Things built up. Only people who have come close to committing suicide know those feelings. For years I had battled the "black dog" but had refused to let myself wallow. This time I felt like my mind was separating from my body. I sought psychiatric assistance, but without medication, and I consulted a lady I knew from the Salvation Army. With her help and the listening ear of the psychiatrist, I embarked on a mixture of rudimentary therapy and a major fourth-step moral inventory. This amounted to a full outpouring about my life, resentments, fears, and anxieties. The loss had triggered a multitude of other unresolved issues and losses, and it was only at that time that I realized they needed addressing. In hindsight it was really only just the beginning.

The true experience of God can be felt only in the heart, I believe, through either circumstances or desire. The juxtaposition of the rational, intellectual life to the desire for a spiritual life was a constant tension at that time as I was seeking God and exploring different denominations. I became drawn to the works of the religious scholar Barbara Thiering, whose work on the Dead Sea Scrolls later led her to claim that the resurrection of Jesus Christ had not taken place.

It was only when I did a religious retreat for the first time, on the recommendation of the woman from the Salvation Army, and was told by the nun who was my spiritual director to meditate on the resurrection, that I had not just another epiphany but a full religious conversion. As described in a Sufi poem, "I opened my eyes and by the light of his face around me . . . only God I saw."[1]

Later I went "church shopping" but found an emptiness in many congregations, and occasional outright unhealthy fanaticism, despite the good intentions I sometimes sensed in the community. The X factor was missing for me. It was in the Catholic Church that I found the sense of mystery and sacramentality that I had experienced during my conversion and that I continually longed for—the symbol of spirituality and God's presence as an answer to the needs of my soul.

Having converted to Catholicism in 1993, I began studying a theology degree part-time. I also subscribed to a British magazine called *The Tablet*, which on one occasion ran a small advertisement for someone familiar with twelve-step recovery programs and Christian spirituality to write a series of books on the subject. To make a long story short, I wrote some ideas on the theme, and that is how *Steps to Life: A Spiritual Journey with Christian Mysticism and the Twelve Steps* began in the 1990s. It was eventually published in Sydney by ABC Books in 2004, and it is now being revised for publication by Loyola Press and rechristened as *Twelve Steps to Spiritual Freedom: Understanding the Christian Roots of Twelve Step Programs*.

The 1990s were a honeymoon period for me spiritually. I felt I was on a call, a mission, and I worked as a hospital chaplain for six years (I am also revisiting that profession as a part-time chaplain at the time of writing). I saw God in the mess. I saw my depression as a spiritual opportunity, a chance to liberate my mind and soul. I believe this happened and continues to happen. Back then, had the priesthood been open to me, I would have considered joining. When everyone else was off getting married, having babies, and climbing the corporate ladder, I was on a spiritual mission. I learned to discern church doctrine from my own spirituality, and I found my own equilibrium in it all. That took time and many inner and outer battles.

As I present this revised edition to you, I am mindful of how my own spiritual life has changed. My prayer life is not what it used to be. What started out as a passionate call is now peaceful and grounded from having weathered the storms of experience, and it is tempered by my own longings, heartaches, and distractions.

As I'm writing this in 2013, it is the thirty-year anniversary of my time in a twelve-step program, the twentieth anniversary of my conversion to Catholicism, and the twentieth anniversary of my sister Rebecca's death. I have also lost several people in my life in the past decade, most particularly a former boyfriend in tragic circumstances, closely followed several months later in 2008 by my spiritual mentor, the former Jesuit father Brian Stoney. (It is to Brian whom I dedicate this book.) In other words, it is a time when much has passed in terms of grief and loss, but also in terms of milestones to celebrate and to bear witness to the graces I have been given.

In twelve-step programs there is the idea that peeling the layers of the onion to free oneself from the "bondage of self" takes an indefinite amount of time. People sometimes experience a significant difference between what they think they desire in life and what life actually unfolds to them. A big chunk of the onion was peeled away during those key turning points for me in the past three decades. I am now reminded of the three key things I need in life—peace, love, and purpose—and how I continually need to bring myself back to those things and make sure they are in harmony. The twelve steps and the Ignatian Spiritual Exercises have helped in that regard, and prayer, meditation, and supportive guidance are what ground me.

At the time of this writing, I am also mindful of how my own world and the world around me has changed since the 1990s, when I penned my first draft of this book. September 11 and the usual suspects of wars, terrorism, and conflict infiltrate daily life, and people are displaced everywhere, literally and, for many in the West, certainly in an emotional or spiritual sense. As my mind goes back to that first experience of the desert in Jordan, I reexperience God in a different way, and in a different world, one driven by fear and uncertainty in many ways but also with a bubbling universal spiritual contagion that moves in various forms, some extreme and potentially dangerous, some not—but moving toward something all the same. Perhaps many are seeking a sense of connection and mystery with the universal whole. The twelve steps are part of that movement and awakening.

I hope this book helps those who have dealt with, or are struggling to deal with, their addictions, life crises, and turning points, and those who are seeking deeper spiritual development. I also hope it helps those seeking to find a path amid the maze of contemporary and traditional religious and spiritual philosophies. In this book, the linking of Christian and especially Ignatian spirituality with the twelve steps, combined with personal lived experience, shows the healing potential of what can happen when two people meet and hear each other's stories. Our stories give us a glimpse of another world, of touching the divine and of seeing through a glass darkly ("We see in a mirror, dimly, but then we will see face to face," 1 Corinthians 13:12). The American writer Raymond Carver writes about the "something" that is glimpsed from the corner of the eye. My own story gave me a glimpse into another world, and I hope that it and all the stories told here do the same for you. (I'm grateful to several friends who have contributed stories that appear at the beginning of several chapters—thank you all.)

Introduction

The Desire for Connection

The call today is to transcend this world of signs and symbols, and enter the new creation, the new world which is revealed in all the great traditions. This is the call of humanity today. We are all involved in it.
—Bede Griffiths[2]

A Movement Begins

On any night in any city in the world, people from all walks of life, of every sex, race, and religion, gather in halls or community centers to meet with those who call themselves "anonymous." These are twelve-step groups, and they might consist of gamblers, alcoholics, drug addicts, or any other group of people seeking recovery from an addiction.

It is no coincidence, and no mean feat, that the spiritual movement of the twelve steps, which began in the 1930s, was conceived when two men both suffering the same problem of addiction got together to help each other. From such small beginnings millions of lives have been transformed.

This movement, which became Alcoholics Anonymous, or AA, gained many of its ideas from the Oxford Group, a spiritual movement that began in 1908, when Frank Buchman, a passionate and ambitious

Lutheran pastor from Philadelphia, experienced a life-changing spiritual transformation while attending a religious convention in Keswick, England. After experiencing a profound sense of spiritual separateness, Buchman allegedly became overwhelmed with the desire to completely surrender to God. This later prompted him to make amends with committee members he had argued with on a settlement house project or a hospice for the poor, back in Philadelphia. He wrote each person:

> Am writing to tell you that I have harbored an unkind feeling toward you—at times I conquered it but it always came back. Our views may differ but as brothers we must love. I write to ask your forgiveness and to assure that I love you and trust by God's grace I shall never more speak unkindly or disparagingly of you.

Each time he wrote a letter, Buchman said he felt it in a new way. "The last line cost me most of all," he said. "I almost wrote it in my own blood."[3]

Eager to share this experience, he began an evangelical group at the nearby Oxford University. What became known as the Oxford Group later spread throughout the world.

The Oxford Group can be seen as the beginning of the worldwide self-help spirituality movement. The movement encouraged people to share their own spiritual journeys and reflect on their inner life, quite a radical thing at a time when the world was dramatically changing. The moral relativism of communism was growing in popularity, and what was perceived to be the old moral order was fading away. In light of Adolf Hitler's rise to power in the 1930s, it is no surprise that the Oxford Group became known as moral rearmament.

The Oxford Group based its support network on "the four absolutes"—love, honesty, purity, unselfishness—and contained many of the elements of Christian spiritual tradition, free of the traditional dogma associated with churches. Like Alcoholics Anonymous (AA), the Oxford Group also involved individuals sharing their different stories. Looking back on this significant history, one of AA's founders, Bill W., later described the Oxford Group as "a nondenominational evangelical movement streamlined for the modern world."[4]

One might say that the seeds of the twelve-step experience were sown when the famous Swiss psychoanalyst Carl Jung met with Rowland H., an alcoholic who was desperately trying to get sober. Jung informed Rowland that in his experience, only those who experienced a dramatic spiritual awakening were able to get sober.

To Rowland, an adamant man of faith, Jung retorted with strong sentiments. He knew the severity of the problem: "ordinary religious faith isn't enough"; a "transforming experience, a conversion experience" was needed to "recognize your personal hopelessness . . . [to] cast yourself upon whatever God you think there is."[5] Rowland thereafter attended the Oxford Group, which in essence had the following teachings:

1. Admit powerlessness in managing one's life.

2. Become honest with self; make an examination of conscience.

3. Make a rigorous confession of personal defects in order to not be alone with problems.

4. Look at distorted relationships and make amends to people wherever possible.

5. Resolve to help others in need without seeking prestige or material gain.

6. Through meditation seek God's direction and help and try to practice these principles of conduct always.[6]

In December 1934, in Towns Hospital, New York, Bill W., a chronic alcoholic, lay in a hospital bed after yet another drinking binge, overcome by the blackest depression he had ever known. Reflecting afterward, Bill W. wrote: "Before the coming of faith I had lived as an alien in a cosmos that too often seemed both hostile and cruel. In it there could be no inner security for me."[7] Fortunately, this blackness was followed by a spiritual experience that changed his life forever—a white-light experience of the Spirit that overwhelmed and liberated him.

On hearing about Bill's spiritual conversion, his doctor, William Silkworth, wisely discerned that Bill had undergone a transformational experience, which could help him with his problem. He assured him that he had not gone mad.

Just before his conversion experience, Bill had been visited by his friend Ebby, who had become an Oxford Group member because of his friend Rowland H. and who gently told him his formula for recovery. Ebby also gave Bill a book, William James's *Varieties of Religious Experience*, which explained that the religious conversion experience had an objective reality.

Several months after his Towns Hospital experience, Bill had an overwhelming desire to drink one night. As fate would have it, he was introduced that night to Dr. Bob S., a surgeon, and alcoholic, from Akron, Ohio. Over long discussions into the night, their mutual need to recover brought them to an understanding that, by synthesizing medical knowledge and spirituality with individual alcoholics' experience, sobriety was possible.[8] In other words, a holistic mental, physical, and spiritual approach to the treatment of alcoholism and a view of alcoholism as a disease or spiritual malady could help people begin the road to recovery and get a new lease on life.

Bill and Bob's early experiences served as the genesis of what some have called the greatest spiritual movement of the twentieth century. Both men set up meeting groups in their respective cities, and slowly the society of Alcoholics Anonymous was born. Over time, Ebby's Oxford Group word-of-mouth teachings helped Bill develop the twelve suggested steps for recovery:

1. We admitted we were powerless over alcohol—that our lives had become unmanageable.

2. [We] came to believe that a Power greater than ourselves could restore us to sanity.

3. [We] made a decision to hand our will and our lives over to the care of God as we understood him.

4. [We] made a searching and fearless moral inventory of ourselves.

5. [We] admitted to God, to ourselves and to another human being the exact nature of our wrongs.

6. [We] were entirely ready to have God remove all these defects of character.

7. [We] humbly asked Him to remove our shortcomings.

8. [We] made a list of all persons we had harmed, and became willing to make amends to them all.

9. [We] made direct amends to such people wherever possible, except when to do so would injure them or others.

10. [We] continued to take personal inventory and when we were wrong promptly admitted it.

11. [We] sought through prayer and meditation to improve our conscious contact with God, as we understood Him, praying only for knowledge of His will for us and the power to carry that out.

12. Having had a spiritual awakening as the result of these steps, we tried to carry this message to alcoholics and to practice these principles in all our affairs.[9]

Eventually, the movement withdrew from the Oxford Group and adopted the name *Alcoholics Anonymous*. By 1939, the book *Alcoholics Anonymous* (known as *The Big Book*), with twenty-eight case histories, was published. In 1989 distribution of the book had totaled eight million copies.[10] According to AA's website, a million copies of the book are distributed every year.

In the traditional understanding of the mythological quest referred to as the hero's journey, the hero is called to transcend his or her ordinary world into another special world, to connect with something larger than him—or herself. The journey began for me when I joined a twelve-step program in the early 1980s, and embarked on a deeper spiritual search in the early 1990s following a breakdown, and in 2009 after losing both my boyfriend and my spiritual mentor the year before.

When I drove out of a retreat in Sydney in the early 1990s, I remember feeling overwhelmed by a new burst of joy and love, a feeling of being in the palm of God's hand and that nothing would hurt me again. This great consolation was not to last, of course, as life dishes up many challenges, but I knew that I had crossed a threshold into a new world, just as I had done in 1983 when I joined a twelve-step program. When I recently did the Ignatian Spiritual Exercises, I remembered intensely that great feeling in that moment of being loved by God.

As the unwitting contributor to the early ideas that led to the formation of AA, Carl Jung wrote in his memoir: "My life is a story of the self-realization of the unconscious." He wisely added, "We are a psychic process we do not control."[11] The big picture of your life is up to God, but the details may be unknown to you. Be assured, you are part of a much bigger process. Jung referred to the power of individuation, as a spiritual force, God's life or spirit coming from the depth of our essential being. In essence, it is our homesickness for God. In a letter to Bill, Jung wrote that Rowland's "craving for alcohol was the equivalent, on a low level, of the spiritual thirst for wholeness, expressed in medieval language: the union with God." Jung added that the only way to process such an experience so that it is not misunderstood in contemporary society is as follows:

> [So] that it happens to you in reality and it can only happen to you when you walk on a path which leads you to higher understanding. You might be led to that goal by an act of grace, or through a personal and honest contact with friends, or through a higher education of the mind beyond the confines of mere rationalism. I see from your letter that Rowland H. has chosen the second way, which was, under the circumstances, obviously the best one.[12]

The quest for truth has always been part of human yearning. As with the turning points in a hero's journey, this search for truth in the spiritual life can lead to an experience of a power outside oneself, sometimes experienced as the Spirit. As Bill W.'s story is testimony to, revelation and new insight are often the beginning of the discovery of such truth. The phrase "the truth will make you free" (John 8:32) becomes a lived possibility when a person embarks on a twelve-step program.

Our desire to transcend who we are is something unique to the human condition, and it can be linked to our desire to connect with the "other." Many people try to find this transcendence with drugs or alcohol or simply by running away from their emotions.

A pertinent idea for those seeking insight from twelve-step programs is that when people are ready to let go of their egos, especially the desire to control (often inspired by the fear of what might happen if things fall apart), they can make this connection and go beyond themselves. A commitment to be open to the Spirit or a power greater than ourselves gives us the potential and courage to face the reality of our true selves, without denial.

Like the hero's journey, pilgrimage is also a key part of the Christian spiritual tradition. Throughout history, Christians have gone on journeys or pilgrimages to holy places, thinking of them as a long trip toward heaven, their "native land." To incorporate the twelve steps into your life means abandoning yourself to a spiritual journey and finding your own native land; it is inevitably a pilgrimage of the heart.

I know many people who have walked the famous Camino de Santiago, or Way of St. James, pilgrimage in Spain, and feel that their life is transformed as a result, despite the fact that it was often a painful process for them. They took their life challenges with them. So it is with this spiritual process. You must be prepared to face fear and abandonment on such a journey, and you will learn to grow in the face of feeling alternatively inspired and desolate, and to hand over your will and life to God and ask the Spirit to guide you. The Benedictine writer Demetrius Dumm describes this process: "The Spirit gives us a sense of confidence now, but at the same time, a deep feeling of homesickness as we yearn for what is still to be realized . . . the full gift in the kingdom."[13]

Through its development of the twelve steps, Alcoholics Anonymous unwittingly tapped into something profound in people's psyche, something about our essence as human beings and the very nature of our spiritual striving. By emphasizing that alcoholism was a threefold illness—spiritual, mental, and physical—AA tapped deep into our need for a holistic approach to resolving our malaise and internal angst. Addiction is not a moral problem; it is a sickness that invades every aspect of a person's being. By emphasizing belief in a God of our own understanding, AA introduced an idea of each of us having a personal image of God, suited to our deep-seated needs.

As we face the complexities of living in the twenty-first century, there is a role for twelve-step programs in the spiritual lives of millions of people. The dualistic framework of traditional religious models no longer fits the spiritual needs of many people. We live in a world that moves fast; constant change is the only certainty. Lack of ritual, a lack of a sense of the sacred, and a general lack of meaning in life have led many people to hunger for spirituality. Today we face ambiguities and uncertainties in our work, the complexities of relationships, the insecurity of the financial world and other institutions. Many of the old institutions of our society, including mainstream religion, are changing and in some cases disintegrating.

Balancing all the competing forces of postmodern life is a challenge for everyone—and depression, suicidality, and other such problems may be partly the result of all this turmoil and lack of connection to the sacred.

The twelve steps offer us enormous hope amid the complexity in our lives. Lack of connection—that feeling of being detached from others and from ourselves—has become part of the human condition. The twelve steps, when integrated with essential elements of the Christian spiritual tradition, can help answer this need we have to connect. The twelve steps are not only a lifeline for those with addictions; they also can be a blueprint for spiritual development. They provide a new focus for self-fulfillment and meaning, and they can fuel a revitalized form of spirituality, one that is free of some of the institutional Church's dogmatic constraints but still able to coincide with the essence of the Gospel and the best that Christianity has to offer. The program also works hand in hand with all the other great religious traditions, as well as for those who do not self-identify as formally religious.

The ancient Greek Heraclitus spoke of the overarching unity in the universe, the *logos*. At the start of John's Gospel in the New Testament, he indirectly refers to this as "the Word"—"In the beginning was the Word, the Word was with God, and the Word was God" (John 1:1). When we can reconnect with and experience this unity, it helps us to find meaning and liberation in our universe and in our lives.

On Mystics

There are many different definitions of *mystic*. Mystics can be those who experience God or the divine, outside the realm of rational or temporal understanding and beyond the traditional understanding of their own religion. They can be those who seek union with God, who, "penetrated with the divine substance," lose themselves, or they can be those who "desire to know, only that they may love." Mystics, above all, desire "union with the principle of things in God." Mystical states, while invariably transient, can result in great insights into truth but cannot always be intellectually comprehended.[14]

As well as addressing my own and other people's stories, this book looks at some of the great Christian mystics, including the Eastern monastic desert father St. Anthony, St. John of the Cross, Julian of Norwich, Mechthild of Magdeburg, St. Francis of Assisi, and St. Ignatius of Loyola. St. Ignatius's mystical spirituality may well have influenced the formation of the twelve steps.

It is important to mention that throughout the history of the Christian tradition, the quest for perfection, originally a Greek idea adopted by the church fathers, has remained paramount. Despite this history, this quest is not integral to having a relationship with God. When this quest takes the form of the twelve steps, it is not about achieving perfection but striving for authenticity. This is a crucial point in the field of spirituality. As the AA *Big Book* says: "We are not saints. The point is, that we are willing to grow along spiritual lines."[15]

Lived action is the embodiment of both our spiritual life and our potential to realize the divine in ourselves. We live this action by changing our behavior through psychological and/or spiritual means, which pays homage to the fact that true faith should liberate us, not constrain us. In other words, lived action should help free you from the bondage of self. This is a true sign of authenticity in the spiritual life.

1

Moments of Truth

Step 1: We admitted we were powerless over alcohol, that our lives had become unmanageable.

Lying there in conflict, I dropped into the blackest depression I had ever known. . . . I cried out, "Now I'm ready to do anything."

—Bill W.[16]

Matt Talbot's Story

It was outside a bar early on a Saturday morning in Dublin 1884 when the twenty-eight-year-old Matt Talbot received the grace to abstain from alcohol for the rest of his life.

Broke and dejected after his friends refused him drinking money, he stood draped around a lamppost for a while and then walked toward the Royal Canal. It was there that he had a conversion experience, a flash of insight. He suddenly saw himself as he really was: rejected, penniless, self-centered, mean, a slave to alcohol.

Later that afternoon Matt went to confession, where he promised to abstain from alcohol for three months. His confessor was wise to the fact that Matt would need special help to remain sober, and he encouraged him to go to daily Mass and Holy Communion, something not even expected of the devoutly religious in those days. Matt went through agonizing alcohol withdrawal on his own—these were the days before AA or detox. Under the guidance of a Jesuit spiritual director, he later underwent an austere routine of prayer, fasting, and theological education.

In 1890 Matt made another pledge to seek Christian perfection and joined the Third Order of St. Francis. His spiritual advisers had chosen a strict rule of the early Irish monasteries: prayer, penance, fasting, work, and study.[17] In this, Matt was not unlike the earliest monastics in the way he went about his spiritual devotion. He also managed to stay sober for the rest of his life. Perhaps what marks Matt Talbot's spiritual journey was his openness to where the Spirit was leading him and his willingness to go to any length.

A Necessary Death

When I joined a twelve-step program in 1983, one of the first experiences I had was what Bill W., Carl Jung, and others have referred to as a psychic shift. I suddenly saw my life and the world around me completely differently. After feeling like a broken mess, I had a sense of hope and purpose. As I began to familiarize myself with the twelve-step program, I could see that something major was happening even though I did not fully understand it. This shift is a continual process that happens when you revisit Steps 1 and 2, but you must trust the process you do not fully understand.

Like Matt Talbot did, to admit complete defeat in any area of life is to let go of the ties that bind. The difference with the psychic shift of this new, special world is that it is so very different from the old way of viewing the world, and it is countercultural in the sense that it involves admitting powerlessness. This shift can occur at any time in life for all kinds of reasons. Feelings of disintegration, despair, loneliness, emptiness, alienation, abandonment, and separation are often the symptoms of a crisis that will lead to a turning point at which you see yourself as you really are. It may be that addiction leads you to that point, or perhaps a breakdown or similar life-shattering experience.

I believe that I am drawn to certain books for a reason. Included among the traditional spiritual writers I am drawn to are Thomas Merton, in particular his diaries, and St. John of the Cross, for his understanding of the dark night of the soul. Among the contemporary writers I am drawn to are the former nun Karen Armstrong's autobiography *The Spiral Staircase*, the actress Mia Farrow's autobiography *What Falls Away*, the Australian terror suspect David Hick's book *Guantanamo: My Journey*, and the tennis player Andre Agassi's autobiography *Open*. All of these writers address a time in their lives when they were in a black hole of despair, a prison, literally or figuratively, from which they did not think they would get out. At the very least they all experienced periods of great internal struggle, depression, doubt, and a feeling of separateness that often overwhelmed them. Ultimately, they grew through those periods in their lives.

In my work as a hospital chaplain I have witnessed that a wound can be a path to wholeness. The founder of the Jesuit order, St. Ignatius, like many people in the hospital facing life-threatening or long-term illness, was forced to reflect on his life after he was wounded as a soldier. He read spiritual books during his recuperation and ultimately experienced a spiritual conversion, where his famous emphasis on "noticing" and awareness of what goes on within, took hold.

As with St. Ignatius of Loyola, sometimes being wounded forces us into self-reflection and acceptance of our powerlessness. I recently watched a few episodes of the Emmy Award–winning television series *Homeland*. In portraying the life of a terror suspect, the series also portrays how, despite the wars all around us that we have no control over, many of us are wounded within. For me the message is clear: only we can address this war within ourselves, this damage within, and ask God for help in doing so.

When Bill W. cried out in Towns Hospital, "I am ready to do anything!" he was in effect taking the first step toward admitting his complete powerlessness and helplessness in the face of his addiction, in the face of his very humanity. Step 1 is about coming to a turning point at which you admit that you are completely powerless and have totally given in. It is saying to your conscious self: "I am totally beaten. I cannot fight this on my own."

Just as it was for Matt Talbot, St. Ignatius, and Bill W., moments of truth can often be life-saving events, because they free us from the bondage of denial and all the emotional energy we need to maintain the facade that everything is OK.

To admit your powerlessness over something is the beginning of the experience of freedom. Doing so is a spiritual experience, since so much of living a spiritual life is about becoming free to be who you really are. Admitting your powerlessness is the beginning of the journey to becoming free of the bondage of self.

Ironically, when you come to the point at which you accept that you are beaten and broken, you become liberated. As the Benedictine writer Demetrius Dumm said, "Bondage alone leads to nothing; bondage acknowledged opens the way to salvation."[18]

When you take the first step, you become a new person. You not only suddenly see yourself as you really are but also discover *who* you really are. You begin to self-integrate and undergo a self-actualization process that will increase your awareness, freedom, and your sense of inter-relatedness and of going beyond yourself.[19]

When you say, "My life is chaos," it may involve giving into that chaos and accepting that you are at rock bottom. But deep within, you are on the verge of completely rearranging your essential self. As Carl Jung stressed to the alcoholic Roland H., emotional rearrangements and displacements take place as you enter into a new way of being.

Often faith stories involve a death and a resurrection. At various times in our lives we face crises that we can work through only by "dying" to our old way of living. These are the moments of truth when we accept that we are beaten or broken; these moments are part of a cycle of death and rebirth, a never-ending spiritual process. We must experience a death of our self in order to live. *Death* can mean loss of spiritual life, the loss of meaning, or the loss of any sense of identity. No matter what it means, though, there is no choice in these situations. You have reached a crossroads.

Our life crises may lead to what the medieval mystic St. John of the Cross called "the long dark night of the soul," but they can ultimately bring us to a revelatory state of spiritual rebirth. These tragic experiences not only open us up for God to come into our lives but also pave the way for us to be introduced to ourselves, "to grow along spiritual lines"[20] in a way that we cannot anticipate. In writing of his experiences in a Nazi concentration camp, the Austrian psychiatrist Victor Frankl said, "Suffering introduces me to myself."[21]

Our Stories

Those people who are in twelve-step programs such as AA and those who are in recovery from addictions who tell others of their experiences remain connected to their story. This helps them to become contentedly free from their addiction and enables them to live a peaceful life.

Bible stories, such as those in the book of Exodus in the Old Testament, tell us how people became disconnected with God when they forgot their story and their "self" took over. The whole idea of remembering who we are is crucial. When we forget who we are or lose sight of our primary faith relationship, we lose focus and fail to stay connected with others. We fail to find meaning in life through a sustaining relationship with God. For example, the "exodus" experience is Israel's story of moving from bondage to freedom. Our own story is also one of God hearing our call and responding out of love: "Out of the slavery their cry for help rose up to God. God heard their groaning,

and God remembered his covenant, . . . and God took notice of them"
(Exodus 2:23–25).

The Israelites' exodus from the bondage of Egyptian oppression was
also when the Israelites first received the "creative call" of the Lord.[22]
For us, this can be seen as the call to respond in our own unique way to
an unknown journey that takes us out of bondage. Our bondage may
be psychological, spiritual, emotional, or a combination of all three.
You might say that we are all born in the bondage of Egypt. We are
called to be free, but realizing that freedom eludes us.[23] To be left
with no hope is spiritual bondage. The prophet Isaiah emphasizes this:
"Then you will say in your heart, . . . 'I was bereaved and barren, exiled
and put away'" (Isaiah 49:21).

The biblical theme of exodus also has a parallel to the desert experience in the Christian tradition. The desert fathers and mothers, who
were the early exponents of monasticism in the first centuries of Christianity, understood the wisdom of being in the desert in order to experience God acutely. Being in the desert, being part of an exodus, is a
metaphor for what you will experience when you enter the wilderness
of the unknown. When you admit your powerlessness, you enter the
"desert"; you let go of attempts to control. The idea of being in total
control as key to a successful life is one of the greatest delusions of
modern society, and it is one of the most powerful delusions of those
who are in the grips of addiction.

Envision Step 1 as a creative act. In admitting your powerlessness,
you become receptive to a voice that calls you to be something beyond
what you are. This in itself requires the creativity and grace of God,
as well as being open to receiving that grace. You cannot control your
addictions or vulnerabilities by yourself. You need help from a higher
power and from others.

A seminal thinker and mystic in the history of early Christianity
and considered one of the first philosophers of the age, Origen

(AD 185–254) was a teacher with the famous Alexandrian school of Greek philosophy. A pioneering humanist, Origen radically believed in the dignity of human beings and that everyone would reach salvation. Proficient in biblical studies and Greek culture, he was also very familiar with the pagan and Jewish worlds, making him a link between faith and culture.

Origen lived during the turbulent times of the Roman Empire. The barbarian invasions were taking place, and Christians were a persecuted sect. Many were martyred. Persecuted and imprisoned before he died, like many others after him, Origen affirmed the church's view that the highest form of spirituality is martyrdom and that any authentic form of spirituality involves some form of death. Thus, he reasoned, asceticism and martyrdom were the keys to spiritual enlightenment.

We might be tempted to condemn Origen's martyrdom as an extreme act of self-denial and a stand against individualism. But instead, see it in a positive light and connect it to Step 1. If you view taking the first step as a "death"—as dying to an old way of being, dying to your old self and to willful attempts to control—then this early Christian idea of asceticism and martyrdom can enhance your spirituality. You can find spiritual life through tragedy. When you die to the old, you begin a transformation process that allows you to bring in the new.

Origen understood that conversion was about the soul returning to God. The conversion process begins with the Spirit stirring up the soul and making it aware of its need for conversion. Origen saw the soul as being on a pilgrimage. Through contemplation the soul eventually comes to experience light, revelation, and knowledge of the Divine.

If you see the spiritual journeying of the twelve steps as a pilgrimage, too, then Step 1 is the beginning of that journey out of the wilderness and toward a spiritual home. We can't avoid this time of being in the wilderness, subject to feelings of complete helplessness. As Origen said: "You must come out of Egypt. . . . Pursue your spiritual journey through the wilderness until you come to the well which the kings dug."[24]

This journey through the wilderness is similar to what happens when you begin a journey with the twelve steps. God has a master plan in your life, which is revealed as time goes along:

> Moreover when the soul sets out from the Egypt of this life to go to the promised land, it necessarily goes by certain roads and . . . observes certain stages that were made ready with the Father from the beginning. . . . [M]y soul has long been on pilgrimage. . . . [W]hen the soul has returned to its rest, that is, to the father land in paradise, it will be taught more truly and will understand more truly what the meaning of its pilgrimage was.[25]

This is the nature of our journey.

The sixteenth-century Spanish Carmelite mystic St. John of the Cross wrote in his famous work *The Dark Night* that the soul should pass through two nights in order to attain union with God (insofar as it is possible in this life) through love. The first night, or "purgation," involves the senses; the second, the spiritual part of the soul.[26]

In his works *The Ascent of Mount Carmel*, John of the Cross talks of an "active" night and a "passive" night.[27] In contemporary terms, we can think of the active night as involving doing certain things to let go of what is unhelpful to you on your spiritual journey. The passive night is God working in you—you do nothing—and it may involve times of feeling sheer emptiness.

John experienced his own "long dark night of the soul" in 1577, when he was unjustly imprisoned for nine months and subjected to physical and mental abuse by members of his own religious order, who may have been threatened by his spiritual influence.[28] Despite this dreadful betrayal, John's acute experience of love, pain, and despair enhanced his understanding of how emptiness, often preceded by purgation, can open us up to God. In times of great suffering, John developed an enormous capacity to love and a more authentic spirituality.

John understood that this journey that takes us beyond self into the "night" is a journey that ultimately brings great gifts. When darkness and pain are present, the love of God is also present, bringing the soul companionship. The "night" can be a journey to truth. Despite the times it may appear to be chaos or abandonment, it can become a space for God to fill.

It is important to note that the idea of the ascent of the soul is an image for spiritual progress. It is not about self-realization via perfection or "being good." It is about union with God. John of the Cross knew that this is the one goal of the spiritual life. He was able to give solace to people such as the grieving mother and widow for whom he wrote the poem "The Living Flame of Love" as his hymn to the Holy Spirit. He understood the paradox that being wounded in some way could make one whole, for he had experienced this firsthand in his own life. Being "wounded" in this sense might mean psychological or emotional scarring, such as the legacy of abuse, depression, loneliness, loss, or weakness.

To admit that your life is unmanageable and that you are completely powerless is a huge step; it is the first step, and it involves leaving the road you know. In "The Ascent of Mount Carmel," John wrote:

> As regards this road to union, entering on the road means leaving one's own road, or better, moving on to the goal; and turning from one's own mode implies entry into what has no mode, that is, God.[29]

Accepting being beaten involves letting go of self. And to let go of self you need to let go of what you know. This is part of the journey toward our more authentic self:

This is so that the really spiritual person might understand . . .
that the more annihilated she be for God . . .
the more is she united with God, and the greater the work
she does.[30]

The journey that begins with Step 1 can become your journey to freedom, but to enter the transformation fully, you need to let go of your obsessions with what is rational and with having control.

Just as they were for Matt Talbot and Bill W., events in our lives can be the beginnings of self-discovery and transcendence. Experiencing Step 1 is to experience a necessary "death" that starts you off on a journey of transformation.

2

The Gradual Awakening

Step 2: [We] came to believe that a Power greater than ourselves could restore us to sanity.

Though I certainly didn't really expect anything, I did make this frantic appeal: "If there be a God, will he show Himself!" The result was instant, electric, beyond description.

—Bill W.[31]

My Story: A Mustard Seed

When I look back at the key turning points in my life over the past three decades, I realize that somewhere in me there must have been a mustard seed of faith, a desire to survive and to break out of my old self—this even though I had no confidence in myself and doubted my own capacity to renew my faith. When I lost the two significant men in my life in late 2008, I was so bereft with grief that I put faith on the back burner. I knew at some deep level, though, that eventually I would be restored. Experience had taught me that. I had overcome other hurdles before.

Now in my hospital work when I bless a stillborn baby, I am mindful of the potential that life carries, of how much hope is invested in that life, and of how devastated we feel when that life is gone. Yet I also see how much beauty and significance accompany the loss of potential beginnings, whether they be lost children or lost loves. We need the ritual and we need to acknowledge our loss, however painful it may be. We need to believe that even though we may not feel it right now, God will restore us back to a place of peace and harmony.

Step 2 is like this. It acknowledges our awareness that however difficult life may be, we will eventually be restored to a state of peace and sanity.

Asking for Help

"Coming to believe" does not necessarily involve intellectual understanding, or any understanding at all for that matter. It can sometimes be a combination of grace, simple heartfelt need, and a desire to change. Asking for help comes with our admission of powerlessness. As Bill W. reflected:

> We have to find a life in the world of grace and spirit, and this is certainly a new dimension for most of us. Surprisingly, our quest for this realm of being is not too difficult. Our conscious entry into it usually begins as soon as we have deeply confessed our personal powerlessness to go on alone, and have made our appeal to whatever God we think there is—or may be.[32]

Becoming open to the workings of Step 2 in your life can also mean becoming aware that a new light has touched you, one that was not there before, or one that you did not know was there before. You will begin to feel connected to yourself and to something outside yourself, to a spiritual presence that acts mysteriously. When you feel this way, you have entered the world of grace and spirit.

As Bill W. experienced, you may have an epiphany, or a holy moment, in which a truth is revealed to you and you suddenly see life in a different way or feel called to adventure. In Step 2 you awaken to the Light, you glimpse something of what you could be, you taste what freedom from self and darkness might be like. The irony is that to experience this freedom, you must first enter the darkness, like someone about to dive into the cavernous depths of the unknown. This is the hard part.

Getting yourself to take the second step may involve calling out to God for help in a crisis, trusting that despite your feelings of fear, all will be well, even if you do not believe in God's existence, or at best, in God's presence in your life. At this point of desperation, you may say something like, "If there is a God, help me!" Or your call to God may be a heart-wrenching plea such as Jesus' at Gethsemane: "Remove this cup from me" (Luke 22:42). When we are in this place, what is clear to us, according to the *Big Book* of Alcoholics Anonymous, is that no human power could relieve our suffering, but God could and would if we call upon him.[33]

For some of us, Step 2 may involve letting go of images of God that are unhealthy or destructive, like a God whom we fear. However you perceive God or a higher power, you need to believe in the unconditional love and acceptance God has for you. This does not involve your natural understanding or knowledge of God. It involves trust and venturing into the unknown. Your personal turning point will transform your present and fill you with hope. The famous Australian writer Morris West expressed this idea very well:

> There comes a moment when you are aware that you are about to step out of light into darkness, out of the knowing into unknowing, without guarantee of return. It is a moment of clearness and stillness, in which you know, with strange certainty, that whatever is waiting to receive you is good, beneficent, loving. You are aware that you have been prepared for this moment, not by any action of your own, but by the gift of life itself, by the nature of life itself. . . .
>
> When, like Lazarus, I was recalled from the darkness, when I stood blinded by the light of a new day, I knew that my life could never be the same again.[34]

This hunger for something, which we all have, is particularly characteristic of Step 2. We may desire to connect in a way that involves seeking out communal support networks, supportive friends, spiritual guides, or counselors. This is particularly so when we are making major changes in our life, such as walking away from a destructive situation.

The eventual revelation of your true self can come about when you let go of your ego. *Ego* in this sense is not to be confused with having healthy self-esteem or "liking yourself." Instead, your ego deludes you into thinking that you can be like God, that you are completely autonomous. Letting go of your ego is in contrast to the idea that you have the power to control everything in your life. It is the ultimate realization that in many areas of your life, when you try to control everything around you, you can fail. Letting go doesn't mean that you become impotent or inactive in the world; rather, it means that you accept what you cannot change, such as certain situations, powerful and overwhelming emotional states, and other people's behavior.

As many people can testify, the price of spiritual development is high. In overcoming your ego, you will often find yourself confronting fear. You may also find yourself overwhelmed by feelings of confusion, hopelessness, extreme emotional pain, or fear of madness. Yet the reality is inescapable: you have to let go of everything you want to cling to in order to experience a spiritual rebirth.

Carl Jung alluded to the idea that humans' spiritual longing is far stronger than our drives for sex or power. Spiritual longing is our ultimate primal longing. In a letter to Bill W. in the early days of AA, Jung wrote:

> I am strongly convinced that the evil principle prevailing in this world, leads the unrecognized spiritual need into perdition, if it is not counteracted either by real religious insight, or by the protective wall of human community.[35]

He also wrote: "Without God, we are all vulnerable. This longing for spirituality is fraught with doubt. We suffer because we are victims of a profound uncertainty."[36]

Part of coming to believe, of being restored to sanity or wholeness on your spiritual journey, is the desire to fill the emptiness, to experience the fullness of reality. The belief that a power greater than yourself may restore you to "sanity" is the beginning.

As I experienced in the key turning points in my life, Step 2 can bring with it the sense that our souls have something in store for us—for "now we see in a mirror, dimly, but then we will see face to face. Now I know only in part; then I will know fully, even as I have been fully known" (1 Corinthians 13:12).

The Christian concept of incarnation is about God entering fully into humanity. In this way, *incarnation* means experiencing the full gamut of the human condition, including emotions at their darkest and their brightest. In daily life, *incarnation* can mean realizing that during life's turning points you are not alone. There is a guiding Spirit outside and acting within you that helps guide you along the way. Suffering is often part of the process, and it is our natural instinct to resist it. But in suffering, you can also see that in the midst of chaos and helplessness there is order.

In the beginning of Genesis, the cosmos is in chaos, but God has a plan. Ultimately, you will also see how sometimes chaos is necessary for God's plan to come to be. I don't mean to suggest that states such as suffering are needed or caused by God. Rather, there is an overarching purpose for us in the world that surpasses suffering.

When I have witnessed great suffering in my work at hospitals, I am often asked, "Why is this happening to me?" I choose to believe that God can bring us some good out of the suffering.

The Gospels emphasize that we must enter into death in order to be reborn or resurrected. In various ways, the journey of Jesus is a story of moving from death to life, of leaving the darkness and emptiness to find meaning and purpose. As with the hero's journey, aspects of Jesus' journey may parallel our own, such as feelings of fear, alienation, and abandonment, or a loss of a sense of order or a sense of self.

For early Christians, "being born from above" in the Spirit through baptism was integral to being a spiritual person (John 3:3). The old person died, and a new person was born; a new identity was formed through a new set of relationships involving church and the communion of the Spirit. The new identity given through the Eucharist (the Christian "breaking of the bread" also known as Holy Communion) is about acquiring eternal life. It gives us a new identity based on new relationships, like the relationship of Father, Son, and Holy Spirit in the Holy Trinity, and it reaches the core of our being. Through grace, which is a gift God gives us freely, not something we earn, Christians are able to become what Christ is by nature.

This gift has tremendous implications for those who are in twelve-step programs. The idea of gaining a new identity and acquiring new relationships through grace is intrinsic to the twelve-step process. The old "addict" self goes through a metamorphosis of sorts in Step 1 and is eventually replaced by the new, more authentic self.

Making that transition from Step 1 to Step 2 requires acknowledging that something outside yourself has come into you. As Paul said in his letter to the Ephesians, "By grace you have been saved through faith, and this is not your own doing; it is the gift of God" (2:8). Paul experienced his own awareness of something coming into him in his own life when, after persecuting Christians with the Romans for many years, he had a sudden and dramatic conversion. He believed he had been saved by grace, and he became a follower of Christ.

Paul's teachings contain many foundational concepts of Christian spirituality. The "new person" appears through letting go of the "old" self: "You were buried with him in baptism, you were also raised with him through faith in the power of God, who raised him from the dead" (Colossians 2:12). Paul also stressed: "You were taught to put away your former way of life, your old self . . . and be renewed in the spirit of your minds, and to clothe yourselves with the new self, created according to the likeness of God in true righteousness" (Ephesians 4:22–24).

If you cling to the old way of being and the behaviors of the past that have not served you and still tell yourself, "This is the way it is," then you stifle the movement of creation in you. What Step 2 challenges you to do is allow things to grow, to move and enter into the new creation. The old order is gone and a new being, you, is there to see (2 Corinthians 5:17). In accepting the challenge, you become part of an eternal process of transformation that has been part of the mystical tradition since pre-Christian times.

In Greco-Roman mythology, transformation is a common theme, such as stories of snakes turning into stones.[37] In such myths, the idea of transformation involved the freeing of the body from the bonds of the material world to bring about a change in spiritual nature, in effect, the making divine of the human being.[38]

In the New Testament, Paul's idea of transformation is similar to that of the Greek and Roman myths. The human being is transformed into the seen image of God. You do not immediately recognize this new reality of being, but it guides your future behavior. This transformation is an invisible process that manifests itself in your life, now. Unlike in the Greek and Roman myths, we cannot bring this transformation about by ourselves; only Christ, God, a higher power, can reshape human beings:

> All of us, with unveiled faces, seeing the glory of the Lord as though reflected in a mirror, are being transformed into the same image from one degree of glory to another; for this comes from the Lord, the Spirit. (2 Corinthians 3:18)

This is a key issue for people in twelve-step programs. Translated to everyday life, this means you cannot totally change yourself. Only through opening yourself to the presence of the Spirit can you undergo this dramatic change—and that requires the grace of God.

3

Letting Go

Step 3: [We] made a decision to hand our will and our lives over to the care of God as we understood him.

> *Take, Lord, and receive*
> *all my liberty,*
> *my memory, my understanding and my entire will—*
> *all that I have and call my own*
> *You have given it all to me.*
> *To you, Lord, I return it.*
> *Everything is yours; do with it what you will.*
> *Give me only your love and your grace.*
> *That is enough for me.*

—St. Ignatius's Prayer[39]

My Story: The Beginning of Faith

When I look back on my journey so far, I see how the intellectual and rational parts of me dominated my thinking and suppressed my deep-seated depression. It took experiences of becoming aware of the Spirit, something completely outside myself, for me to change, to reach a turning point, and that enabled me to live from the heart.

As I've already mentioned, I had battled depression on and off for years. Years of not listening to what was in my heart had taken its toll, and a pervading darkness took root within me. I had walked away from a relationship, lost a potential baby, and isolated myself from many friendships. My self-esteem had eroded over many years.

I became plagued with thoughts of suicide, and I felt totally helpless in the face of them. I often asked myself, "What can I do? If my life has no meaning, if I have no real purpose, why am I here? What is the point of it all?" I felt powerful, dark forces pushing me to the edge. My thoughts of suicide were no longer thoughts; they had become plans.

I felt like my mind was separating from my body. In that inevitable downward spiral I could see myself spinning totally out of control. I felt completely irresponsible for my actions. Part of me felt completely insane. I knew it was only a matter of time before things would go either one way or the other. I have heard many people who have attempted suicide speak of this phenomenon.

Later, after managing to tell a counselor all the truth of my life, all the pent-up anger and feelings of loss, shame, and betrayal, I came to feel a peaceful, reassuring presence envelop me.

I took the plunge and did a silent retreat for five days. I was told to meditate on the resurrection of Jesus, something I had never had much interest in and always had a great deal of difficulty understanding on an intellectual level. What did "raised from the dead" mean, anyway?

What resulted was an awakening of my heart, a spiritual experience in which I experienced a total conversion. It was not unlike the experience of Bill W. It felt like the wind, like the Spirit coming into my soul and body. I was totally changed. I walked away from that experience a completely different person. I still had the same problems, but I had no expectations about my future and I was filled with enormous joy. It was almost as if nothing could ever hurt me again—which of course was not the case, but that's what it felt like. So in effect, my counselor was right: I had to be born again, like Nicodemus in the New Testament, and that meant nothing less than being born in the Spirit.

In that transformational moment, God was at the center of everything. I felt connected. For hours after that, I felt a total surrender, as if I saw only God. It's no surprise that life has never been the same since.

When I recently did St. Ignatius's Spiritual Exercises in my daily life, I was asked in the first week to contemplate the idea of remembering being loved. The memory of my spiritual conversion while I was on retreat came back to me. I remembered driving out of the retreat center feeling overwhelmed by a gust of joy and love, feelings of being in the palm of God's hand and of nothing being able to hurt me again, cocooned in God's love, or a great "consolation," as Ignatius would say. Of course, looking back, those feelings did not last. On reflection during the Spiritual Exercises, I realized that I had been open then to love and to letting go, regardless of the consequences.

In that same year, 1993, my sister Rebecca died tragically while under anesthesia. She had had a complicated mental health history, as well as undiagnosed leukemia and a rare genetic disorder, discovered only after her death. I had gone into pastoral care work in a major Sydney hospital shortly before she died, and I was unprepared to deal with my own grief at that time. In the zeal of ministry and a renewed sense of Step 3, I put my loss on hold. It was, of course, to emerge later on.

What I realize looking back is that I eventually heard the call to conversion and responded. Despite carrying all my life baggage with me, I embarked on the journey; I took the path of faith. Despite the highs and lows over the years, and the moments of doubt in my faith, I have never regretted it.

Opening the Door

Many spiritual writers have reflected on how suffering can bring us closer to God and open us up to the workings of the Spirit. Whatever demons you are battling, be they addictions or meltdowns, all the will and determination you have will result in nothing. The only way through the problem, out of the desolation, is to hand over control of your life to a higher force and to realize that the force—God—is the only thing that can turn around your life. Your only hope is this loving God, whom you may not understand but who is there for you.

Step 3 opens the door to us and brings about a gradual openness and willingness to allow our true self to emerge with the help of God. Essentially, this new journey is the beginning of our search for unity and wholeness. It is also the beginning of freedom: "The more we become willing to depend upon a Higher Power, the more independent we actually are."[40]

You are more connected to human beings when you are more open to others and more able to let go of the fear of what might happen if you fall apart. Thus, your prayer might be:

> God, I offer myself to thee, to build with me and to do with me as thou wilt. Relieve me of the bondage of self, that I may better do Thy will. Take away my difficulties, that victory over them may bear witness to those I would help of Thy power, Thy love, and Thy way of life. May I do your will always.[41]

This prayer from Step 3 of Alcoholics Anonymous, similar to St. Ignatius's prayer at the beginning of this chapter, is the ultimate in letting go with love and gratitude. Ignatius's prayer, which is often prayed during the third week of the Ignatian Spiritual Exercises, like the prayer in AA's Step 3, involves completely handing over your life to God and responding to God from the heart.

Those who have experienced abandonment, helplessness, or despair know only too well that to hand one's life over to God completely carries with it a sense of entering into the unknown as well as relief. Entering into the unknown can be a fearful proposition, but going back to where you have come from is unbearable, however familiar it may be. Your calling is to press forward into the unknown, without expectations, knowing that you are consciously choosing God. In Step 3 you may glimpse the fact that the quality of your life depends on the quality of your relationship with God. Even if you have only a mustard seed of faith, that seed helps feed your soul.

This conscious choice for God in the circumstances of an unknown future is the crux of a spiritual life. The choice forces you to let go of expectations, and it can awaken your heart to love, allowing you to be reborn in the Spirit. As Jesus tells Nicodemus:

> "Very truly, I tell you, no one can see the kingdom of God without being born from above. . . . 'You must be born from above.' The wind blows where it chooses, and you hear the sound of it, but you do not know where it comes from or where it goes. So it is with everyone who is born of the Spirit."
>
> —John 3:3–9

The idea of a pilgrimage of the soul is one that affected both early monasticism and later spirituality in the Middle Ages. It involved the idea of moving away from your "home," a place of comfort in the spiritual sense, to a place you do not know.

The essence of pilgrimage is prayer. Your prayer life, which you begin in Step 3 of twelve-step programs, is really a pilgrimage to your own center, a journey to your heart, a place you do not yet fully know. Embarking on Step 3 is a pivotal part of your pilgrimage, of your twelve-step journey.

An essential part of the Christian concept of moving away from an old way of life to a new way of life through the action of God is the idea of withdrawing into oneself for contemplation. Contemplation was establishing itself during the time of Christ, particularly among some monastic Jewish sects. Later in the Christian tradition, particularly from the time of St. Augustine in the late fourth century, up until at least the twelfth century, the concept of a threefold withdrawal underpinning the spiritual life was popular. The withdrawal involved withdrawing from the world, and withdrawing within the self, in order to experience God above the self—that is, going into the self to go above the self to go beyond the self. People such as the philosopher Origen and the desert fathers of Egypt also embraced this idea. It has been absorbed in the contemplative tradition for centuries, and contemplation is still with us.

The desert as a secluded wilderness where we face both our unknown selves and our unknown future has always been part of Christian spirituality. When I think of the desert, I think of Jesus' experience there, and of my own experience in Amman. Space and emptiness can open us up to God; it was in the desert that Jesus faced temptation by the devil. With its vastness and emptiness, the desert calls to mind the solitary nature of the individual spiritual journey. In the desert you confront your own emptiness and fear, and you find yourself face-to-face with the awesome Mystery that cannot be named or understood. You are forced to rely on God, the God of your own understanding.

The roots of monasticism lie in the Egyptian desert in the fourth century. There the way of life of the desert fathers and mothers was "being" through contemplation and action; in other words, it was a way of life that was "caught" rather than "taught."

These people laid down some essential tenets of Christian spirituality that remain with us today, ideas such as renouncing the world, letting go of ego, letting go of self, suffering as part of life, and preparing to journey with God. For them, the desert took on the most real and stark dimensions. They possessed an all-too-vivid awareness of the evil that exists in the world and a preparedness to combat it. Despite that, they possessed the virtues of humility and charity.

A discussion of monasticism must include the man considered the founder of it, St. Anthony of Egypt. Often called "the father of Christian monasticism," Anthony's story embodies the emptying of self that is involved in going into the desert. In AD 269, at the age of twenty, he responded to Matthew 19:21—"If you wish to be perfect, go, sell your possessions and give the money to the poor, and you will have treasure in heaven; then come, follow me"—by going out into the Egyptian desert and living as a hermit.

In seeking perfection, Anthony renounced his inheritance, lived on the desert margins of a village, and sought guidance from other holy men, becoming renowned as a healer. Anthony epitomized "letting go absolutely." Some of his calls were extreme:

> Hate the world and all that is in it. Hate all peace that comes
> from the flesh. Renounce this life, that you may be alive to
>   God. . . .
> Suffer hunger, thirst, nakedness. . . . [T]est yourselves.[42]

Anthony's values, such as renouncing earthly attachments, apply to today's world, as well: we should not place our material or other attachments, the cares of this world, before our relationship with God. We might interpret his message today as "Be in the world but not of it."

The idea that the monks were engaged in a spiritual "battle" in the desert was not so naive. In fighting the battles within themselves, fighting their own passions and recognizing their own struggles and brokenness, they were able to become closer to the reality of themselves. In today's world, we do not necessarily engage in such a fight. For example, we do not demonize normal parts of our humanity, like sexuality, as the monks did. Their message for today's world can be paraphrased as:

Do not be a mental and emotional slave to your possessions and desires. Instead, strive for emotional detachment from them. Let your desire for truth and closeness to God be your primary focus.

The monastics believed strongly in compunction, an anxiety of one's spirit, a piercing in their hearts that made them aware of their sinfulness and need for mercy. Compunction was often followed by repentance. Hence the desert was a place of freedom but also a place of conflict within the self. The monks' "demons," be they real or imagined, visualized or internal, spurred on the monks to be "stripped of all things" and to be led closer to God. Dealing with inner conflicts enhanced and strengthened their spiritual awareness, furthering them along their journey toward intimacy with God. While the idea of compunction may seem dramatic and extreme, it was perhaps a wise move away from the rationalization of the Greek world, which focused on independent intellectual interpretation of the empirical world. A writer of the times observed of these people: "It is clear to all who dwell there, that through them the world is kept in being."[43]

In today's world, a crisis, a personal breakdown, or a traumatic experience might bring us face-to-face with our own "desert" experience, stripping us "of all things." Such a turning point might cause us to be more honest with someone else or with ourselves about what is really going on in our life, and so at a later period bring about greater spiritual awareness.

In the rational world of today, remember Christ's dictum, "Strive first for the kingdom of God and his righteousness, and all these things will be given to you as well" (Matthew 6:33)—or his words that give us guidance: "When the Spirit of truth comes, he will guide you into all the truth" (John 16:13). Or in twelve-step terms: "See to it that your relationship with him is right, and great events will come to pass for you and countless others."[44]

This all means that when a spiritual relationship is your primary focus, life's other problems are easier to manage. You are not in any way immune from suffering, but you are able to place greater meaning on the bigger picture of your life, and by combining prayer and action, you are bestowed with a greater capacity to deal with problems.

Another famous monastic worthy of attention is St. Benedict, considered the father of Western monasticism. Sent from Umbria to Rome as a young man to study, Benedict was repelled by the goings-on in the city, and he sought solitude by fleeing to a cave in the town Subiaco, where he lived a hermit's life for three years. Encountering much hostility and jealousy from those clerics and others in the church who were threatened by him, because of the large number of disciples who flocked to him, he was forced to make several moves, and he ultimately founded a monastery on the summit of Monte Cassino in 525.

Benedict's "rule" for monastic life has had a dramatic influence on Christian spirituality. However, unlike the extreme asceticism of the desert mothers and fathers, the monasticism espoused by St. Benedict advocated balance while still maintaining the essential monastic virtues of daily prayer, singleness of heart, and humility. The beginning of the prologue of the *Rule of St. Benedict*, a book compiling his rules for monastic life, parallels Step 3 of twelve-step programs in its emphasis on letting go of self: "If you are ready to give up your own will, once and for all . . . and in the Prayer too we ask God that his 'will be done' in us" (Matthew 6:10).

Benedict emphasized the constant ideal of conversion and contemplation: a gradual turning toward God as both a continual goal and continual sustenance. The Benedictine rule echoes how you grow and find true self-fulfillment, by heightening awareness of Christ within: "Let us open our eyes to the light that comes from God, and our ears to the voice from heaven that every day calls out this charge: If you hear his voice today, do not harden your hearts."[45]

By moving beyond what is comprehensible, you get to the unknown, where God lives. Later mystics, such as the anonymous author of the classic work *The Cloud of Unknowing*, understood this. To know God mystically through love, we must abandon what our imagination and preconceived ideas about God tell us. John of the Cross understood that prayer and emptiness, through the *via negativa*, or "the path of nothingness," were a way to God.

When you start your pilgrimage of the heart in Step 3, you are moving from the known to the unknown. You are attempting to empty yourself of all previously held ideas that have not served you. For example, you might need to let go of a cynical attitude or a "me against them" outlook toward the world. Alternatively, you might need to let go of constantly distrusting those closest to you so that you can live more freely. The *Big Book* offers an important maxim on this issue: "Some of us have tried to hold onto our old ideas, but the result was nil until we let go absolutely."[46]

The only way to deal with both suffering and joy is to enter into both with faith, to walk with them, knowing that God is with you. This is what can bring you the connectedness you long for; the lack of that connection can bring on so many ills, such as depression and mental illness.

To walk in the mystery of the spiritual life means to walk in uncertainty, but it is the path of true faith. The prophet Isaiah reminds us of the bigger picture of mystery in our lives: "Do not remember the former things, or consider the things of old. I am about to do a new thing; now it springs forth, do you not perceive it?" (Isaiah 43:18–19).

4

Looking at the Past

Step 4: [We] made a searching and fearless moral inventory of ourselves.

Jesus said, "If you bring forth what is within you, what you have will save you. If you do not have that within you, what you do not have within you [will] kill you."

—Gospel of Thomas[47]

Brian's Story

"If I cannot begin to know myself, I cannot begin to heal myself, so the basic step of this self-knowledge begins with a material confession. Before I confess to anyone else, I must confess to myself—who I really am, what my fears are, and so on. So if I am to put my well-being above everything else, I must start with a concrete list of 'symptoms' to deal with.

"I came from a poor home on the unfashionable side of town, and I had a violent, alcoholic father. I used humor to cope with pain for most of my life.

"For me Step 4 was ridding myself of a yoke across my shoulders. I experienced immense relief. It was as though a huge burden had been lifted from me. I regained a spring in my step. After I had listed all my concrete resentments, I realized the burden I was carrying was my toxic shame and secrets."

Humility and Honesty

What does a fearless and thorough moral inventory involve? Moral inventory is an examination of the nature of what truly drives us, those things that cause behaviors that do not serve us, for example, fear and resentment.

In essence, honesty, an essential part of humility, is the key. Fundamentally, Step 4 is about getting to know your own weaknesses and strengths, your true motives and drives. It is also the beginning of becoming aware of how admitting these things can strengthen and free you.

Step 4 involves asking God to remove whatever has blocked you from connecting with God.[48] Today therapists may talk about this in terms of "toxic shame" or "secrets," those events that fill you with guilt or shame and those things that dominate your life now, regardless of whether or not you were once responsible for them. Step 4 is also about letting go of inordinate or disordered attachments, which are the obsessive attachments to people, places, and things that keep us in bondage.

All this takes humility and honesty, a willingness to see yourself as you truly are. And it leads to a greater capacity to let go of self and become less self-centered, which is an essential part of any authentic spiritual process. Once you deal with the things that separate you from God, the closer you get to your more authentic self.

Step 4 is parallel to the Christian idea of compunction, the earlier monastics' feeling of their heart being pierced, making them aware of their faults and the potential to be free of those faults. For many people, a similar feeling occurs after Step 3, when—yes—there is spiritual peace and commitment, but there is also an awareness of the conflicts within the self that remain. It is during Step 4 that these issues are addressed.

This process of taking a moral inventory, which is often best written down, may lead to confession, formal or informal, or to Step 5, during which you tell someone else the story of your life, how it has been for you, who has hurt you, and how you have reacted. Also, though, a moral inventory can be as simple as asking God to help you become aware of the distortions of your life and to help you to let go of them.

In Step 4, we specifically look at things like fears, resentments, and misdirected instincts. Misdirected instincts include those drives within us for personal recognition or power, or fight-or-flight behaviors that cause us to fluctuate between the constant desire to satiate our ego and low self-esteem. We look at where we have tried to rely on personal empowerment to no avail: "We reviewed our fears thoroughly. We put them on paper, even though we had no resentment in connection with them. We asked ourselves why we had them. Wasn't it because self-reliance failed us?"[49]

Those who are on the verge of completing this step may experience intense feelings of desolation, despair, or anxiety. To admit your own past failures or weaknesses, or your reaction to those of others and their effect on you, can be a daunting process. Yet desolation can play a crucial role in your spiritual growth, by emptying you and making you more vulnerable and open to the work of God.

It is important to remember that the spiritual life is not necessarily about denial of any kind or about forfeiting your humanity in any way. In a spiritual life you need to embrace all aspects of yourself. After all, incarnation is about the Word made flesh, God in the form of humanity. Remember that Jesus Christ emptied himself like a slave (Philippians 2:6–11).

The contemplative tradition stresses renunciation and detachment as part of the path toward illumination and union with God, and these things can be helpful for a contemporary spiritual journey, particularly for those in twelve-step programs. You need to try to release yourself from things such as destructive self-will in order to progress in a spiritual life. By letting go of the attachments that hold back your spirit, you give your heart more freedom.

The moral inventory taken in Step 4 of twelve-step programs is also similar to St. Ignatius of Loyola's "examination of consciousness." As mentioned previously, as a soldier, St. Ignatius was wounded in a siege in the Spanish town of Pamplona in 1521 and taken to the castle of Loyola to recover. It was during his long convalescence, when he read *A Life of Christ and the Saints*, that he experienced a spiritual conversion. His period of penance, meditation, and revelation led him to devise the Spiritual Exercises. Ultimately, he founded the Jesuit order, which aims to serve people and lead them to God, and in particular aims at self-conversion, leading to the service of others.

When practicing the Ignatian Spiritual Exercises in daily life, you combine spiritual awareness in prayer and contemplation, and you examine your consciousness and your day. The Exercises extend over four weeks. The first week involves attending to the "mystery of salvation," which can be understood as acknowledging your own failures and frailties, as well as the gift of God's mercy. The second week involves attending to the life of Christ up to his entry into Jerusalem on Palm Sunday (a deeper process of moral inventory). The third week attends to Christ's Passion, or his suffering and death. This week involves meditating on those things that have emerged from your moral inventory and how they have affected your life. The fourth week focuses on Christ's resurrection and ascension,[50] and in this week, out of the love you have received, you resolve to give yourself totally to God.

Ignatius defines "spiritual exercises" as any method of examining your consciousness—meditation, contemplation, mental or vocalized prayer, or any other method of handling your spiritual life. Spiritual exercises call the soul to remove its unhealthy obsessions, to seek and find the will of God in managing life, and to find your role in the Paschal Mystery (the life, death, and resurrection of Christ).[51] It is easy to envision Steps 4 and 5 of twelve-step programs as similar to Ignatius's exercises.

In Step 4, we ask for God's grace to come and help us during this step, reminding ourselves that God's grace is the action of God lovingly desiring a response from us. Often writing things down is the best way to do this—and as someone who has kept a journal for the past thirty years, I recommend doing so.

Ignatius talks about a five-step plan that is part of an "examination of consciousness." First, you thank God for the good things in your life. Second, you ask God's help to know what your personal failures or weaknesses have been. Third, you pray that you are able to acknowledge your own character weaknesses regularly, in word and deed. Fourth, you ask for God's mercy for these faults in thought, word, and deed. Last, with God's grace, you plan some program of reparation for these things, closing with a prayer such as the Our Father.[52] The last two steps parallel what you aim to achieve in Step 5, discussed in the next chapter.

Ignatius mentions that a confession, a tangible expression of God's forgiveness as happens in the Catholic tradition, may be a good way of completing this examination of consciousness, although it is not essential (a confession is similar to what happens in Step 5). This is because spiritual confrontation can cure our apathy and hearten us in our progress in the spiritual life.[53]

In my pastoral encounters I often find that naming things that people might feel guilty about and encouraging them to take that guilt to God and allow God to hold it with love, and without judgment, helps them. People are responsive and can hear the potential for emotional and spiritual healing when they are in the right relationship with God in their hearts.

Letting go of obsessive attachments may be difficult, and we may never do so completely. Many of us have baggage from our own life experience, such as our childhood, that we carry with us. Loneliness, repressed anger, and shame are some other examples. The things that have caused you great conflict, that have separated you from God in the past and that have the potential to separate you from God now are worthy of attention.

The two key concepts of desolation and consolation are common to Ignatian spirituality and the twelve steps. Spiritual desolation is a state in which you feel lacking in faith, hope, or love. It may involve feeling depressed or being in a state of darkness, turmoil, or restlessness, although not necessarily. It can also bring a brief feeling of deceptive satisfaction, if you succumb to acts like promiscuity or gambling, in an attempt to feed the emptiness. Ironically, spiritual desolation is often followed by feelings of increased emptiness. In contrast, consolation is when you feel stirred in your soul to love for God, and others, for their own sake and no other reason.[54] Both states, desolation and consolation, have three characteristics in common: the feeling itself, such as feeling either distressed or peaceful; the source of the feeling, such as a situation or perhaps God; and the consequences of that feeling in your life, such as a movement toward God or away from God.

Before, during, or after Step 4, you may feel either one of these states. In desolation, you may have anxiety about the nature of the material you will share with others or a feeling of worthlessness or emptiness. In consolation, you may feel peace and love for God. Alternatively, you may feel sadness, which is appropriate, such as when you look at times you have harmed yourself or others. Ignatius refers to this state of consolation as "spiritual excitement of soul."[55]

In my experience, greater insight comes with greater faith. The first time I completed Step 4 in the mid-1980s, it was fairly simple. I did not have the insight that came to me in the following decades. Yet I did my best, and I was as honest as I could be at the time.

When I completed the Ignatian Spiritual Exercises in daily life, they involved the themes of "progress in divine love," "remembering love," "dwelling in love," "love at work," and "receiving and giving love." I had to look at where God had been active in my daily life, and at my interior movements toward and away from God that occurred in different ways. I specifically looked at the movements of consolation and desolation in my daily life.

I became aware of how easily distractions could lead to moments of desolation in my day. This could include having feelings brought about by irritating people, wanting things to be different, or not accepting where I was at in my life.

When I met my spiritual mentor, the former Jesuit Brian Stoney, in the mid-1990s, he had a great effect on my life. He worked and lived with people living on the street in the inner city, had an enormous love for St. Ignatius, and paid homage to the idea that Christ was truly present in the broken. He was my closest male friend as well as my spiritual mentor.

As I engaged in the Ignatian exercises, I experienced consolation and desolation in my day, but I also remembered Brian's enormous reassurance and love. I remembered how he told me to take all my concerns, all the messy parts of my life—the good, the bad, and the ugly—to the foot of the cross and to God. His ability to "read my mind" in a spiritual sense, and his understanding of the forces that were really driving me when I took issues to him, was quite unique, and it is a reason I have referred to him as "the father of my soul" (apparently the term of endearment St. Teresa of Ávila used when referring to her spiritual mentor, St. John of the Cross).

Brian died in a hospice, and when I went to see him just before his death, his speech was slurred as a result of his illness, and it was very frustrating for both of us. Yet I knew he was ready for death, ready to meet God.

When contemplating his death during the Spiritual Exercises, I experienced an enormous sense of loss, because he was no longer in my life. Yet during prayer later in the day, I felt much calmer, embalmed with a sense of love and gratitude for having experienced such a bond with someone, someone who knows you truly, and especially all of your deep, dark secrets. I sometimes still feel his presence guiding me.

Ignatius advises against making major decisions when you are in a state of desolation. Often, such times are instead a call to engage in deeper prayer for guidance.[56] It is not hard to see why. Feelings of intense despair or hopelessness can easily distort your reason. For example, you may want to end a relationship or a positive work opportunity because your state of desolation has distorted your perception of those situations. It is best in this case to wait until you have discussed with a friend, confessor, or a Step 5 participant what course of action, if any, you should take.

One way of dealing with the psychological resistance you might feel before completing Step 4 is to do what Ignatius suggests for those embarking on major life-changing decisions. Imagine being on your deathbed and confessing the truth of your life. What would you say?[57]

In engaging in a fearless and thorough inventory, it is important to remember several things. John of the Cross reminds us that only God is able to comprehend those aspects of our humanity that lie deep within us, unfathomed. If you find yourself besieged by any feelings of discomfort or desolation, you might remind yourself of these words of his: "To come to the knowledge you have not, you must go by a way in which you know not."[58]

Successfully completing Step 4 involves being open to the movement of your heart and to God's grace. If you are on the verge of beginning Step 4, you may feel chaotic, fearful, or reluctant to go forward, but this is where trust comes in. If it were not for life's crises, difficulties, addictions, and so on, that come upon us, there would be no need for this step. As the Old Testament says, sometimes you find yourself afflicted, so that what is in your heart might be made known. This follows on to the desert experience:

> Remember the long way that the LORD your God has led you these forty years in the wilderness, in order to humble you, testing you to know what was in your heart. . . . He humbled you by letting you hunger, then by feeding you with manna, with which neither you nor your ancestors were acquainted, in order to make you understand that one does not live by bread alone, but by every word that comes from the mouth of the LORD. (Deuteronomy 8:2–3)

The fourth-century ascetic monk John Cassian, one of the great monastics, followed in the footsteps of his master, Evagrius (a disciple of the Eastern desert tradition), in perceiving the monk's way of life as an inner journey. That journey begins with beholding God with awe, and it passes through compunction to reach renunciation of self. In this inner life, the monastic's goal is singleness of heart, seeking only God. In carrying out this goal, simplicity and humility are the foundation stones.[59]

Both the Ignatian Spiritual Exercises and traditional Mass mention transformation of the heart. You do not need to be Catholic, or even Christian, to appreciate this idea. It is with this transformation, this purity of heart, that you should approach Step 4, and later Step 5—with a friend, a spiritual guide, a priest, or an adviser. For these steps will bring you further along the road and open you up to how the grace of God will change your life forever.

5

The Old Self Stripped Away

Step 5: [We] admitted to God, to ourselves, and to another human being, the exact nature of our wrongs.

"If you continue in my word, you are truly my disciples; and you will know the truth, and the truth will make you free."

—John 8:31–32

David's Story

"Seeing a therapist enabled me to sort out what were my issues and what were the issues of other people—what I needed to let go of and what I needed to strive toward. Often, I realized that my perceptions were distorted, that I was often overcome with feelings of resentment and paranoia, particularly in regard to what other people thought about me. Again self-centeredness reared its ugly head.

"However, I still needed to address where I had acted out of rage and hurt toward other people. I realized that often I had projected my own shame onto other people in those circumstances.

"I needed to be prepared to sort out what were natural responses to the abusive behavior of others, and to acknowledge where I was hurt or angered by that behavior. Once I had tried to address that, then I could move on from it.

"I also learned to be careful not to suppress anger but rather to acknowledge it and grow beyond it, to work through it and not be dictated by it in other words. Trying to suppress anger, I realized, could be a self-destructive thing, while acknowledging it, along with fear and resentments, helped free me from my bonds."

Crossing the Threshold

Realizing and naming your own wounds is part of the journey to becoming whole. It is part of crossing one of the first major thresholds of a spiritual journey. This is Step 5, a step that can open you up to receive love into your life, particularly the love of a power outside yourself. As St. John of the Cross's poem "The Living Flame of Love" testifies:

> Flame alive compelling,
> yet tender past all telling,
> reaching the secret center of my soul!
> Since now evasion's over,
> Finish your work, my Lover,
> Break the last thread, wound me and make me whole![60]

To admit faults or defects (those personality characteristics that have caused you problems in life), or to admit how you really feel about what has happened in your life, requires that you deflate your ego.

Deflating the ego is another way of saying that you let go of self-will. Self-will is not looking after yourself or self-love; rather, it is the delusion of your mastery over the world and over your life. It is ego-based behavior that excludes God and blocks you off from the light of God by leading you to believe that personal empowerment alone is the key to happiness. The Serenity Prayer gives reassurance during Step 5, for you know you cannot change the past, only the here and now:

> God grant me the serenity,
> to accept the things I cannot change,
> courage to change the things I can,
> and the wisdom to know the difference.[61]

You might feel in Step 5 that the Spirit is calling you to some greater good. In effect, God is calling you in love toward your truth. If you have lived far apart from your truth, then Step 5 can turn things around. Letting go of your ego, which stops you from looking at the truth, is a start. The gradual movement of your heart, the conversion toward life, is what is happening in this step.

As David's story shows, a "shadow history" is the side of yourself that you might not have been aware of before, such as your ego disguised in the form of altruism. By discovering your shadow history in Step 5, you become more integrated, whole, grounded and more discerning in finding out where God is leading you. It is all part of becoming free of the ties that bind you.

There can be a certain security in harboring old resentments or acting out of fear, because doing so is familiar. Hopefully, you can address these things in Step 5. You can look at what is really going on in your heart and what has held you back in life, and perhaps what has caused you to sabotage yourself.

Your inability to address your authentic self can lead to spiritual impoverishment. The non-canonical Gospel of Thomas (part of the Gnostic Gospels discovered in the twentieth century) offers an important message in this regard:

> Jesus said, ". . . the [Kingdom] is inside you and outside you. When you know yourselves then you will be known, and you will understand that you are children of the living Father. But if you do not know yourselves, then you live in poverty and you are the poverty."[62]

In the context of AA, Bill W. reiterated this point:

> I must look inside myself, to free myself. I must call upon God's power to face the person I've feared the most, the true me, the person God created me to be. Unless I can or until I do, I will always be

running, and never be truly free. I ask God daily to show me such a freedom![63]

As you complete the process of revealing yourself to another person through some form of confession or reconciliation—remember that you may see things about your life at certain times and not at others. Other issues may present themselves at a later date, so don't try to be a perfectionist, just be honest. You cannot address all your life problems at once. You can only look at what you need to address in your life now, what has come up for you.

St. John of the Cross emphasizes this need to progress in your spiritual life at your own pace. In your dialogue with God, God treats you "with order, gentleness, and in a way that suits the soul," "little by little," and "carries each person along a different road."[64]

To reconcile with another person means to make things right. In the process of reconciliation of Step 5 you are dealing with the nature of your wrongs, what is truly behind your actions, not with a litany of sins and misdemeanors. During Step 5, you need to watch out for misdirected guilt, that is, over scrupulous guilt about things you may have done. Instead, you should look at what lies behind your misdirected instincts. The force you often discover behind your actions is fear, often fear of abandonment.

In taking on Step 5, you may come up against feelings of fear or desolation as you reveal yourself to another. Step 5 begins by asking God to "remove our fear and direct our attention to what He would have us be. At once, we commence to outgrow fear."[65]

The need for self-knowledge can be powerful. By telling another person about your deepest defects, the things that really disturb you, such as distressing and humiliating memories or secrets, you allow yourself the opportunity to find relief from the anxiety, remorse, and depression that these things have caused in your life. A sensitive spiritual adviser, sponsor, or confidant may help with this process, but ultimately it is in the hands of God. You know only that you have begun your liberation from the bondage of self.

Often, Step 5 is about emerging from isolation, feeling at one with God, with others, and with yourself, for perhaps the first time in your life. Not only does this step often open up the channels of forgiveness; it also has the potential to give you feelings of true kinship with God. How can you quantify such an amazing feeling? At this point, you face the deep divisions within your soul and embark further on a process of finding unity and wholeness—and that requires truly letting go.

When I completed the Ignatian Spiritual Exercises in daily life I reflected on my own conversion experience and how it came about after meditating on the mystery of the resurrection. I remembered I was open to love and keen to let go and experience whatever happened. As Brian's story in Step 4 and David's story in Step 5 demonstrate, making "a material confession" is to put everything on the table before God.

While I was doing the Ignatian exercises, I read the Scripture passage of the Samaritan woman at the well, and I remembered that as I got to know my spiritual mentor, Brian, our relationship reminded me of that same story. Jesus meets the Samaritan woman without judgment, not fazed by her checkered past, and wanting to share the "living water" with her: "[He] told me everything I have ever done," she says (John 4:29). I felt heard and understood by Brian; I could tell him anything. That is a very rare bond, and I realize now how precious and sacred it was.

Steps 4 and 5 are steps of moral inventory, and they parallel the Ignatian exercises closely. Because of that, St. Ignatius's approach may be helpful for those who want to go deeper into this process of moral inventory. In the first week of the Spiritual Exercises, you ask for God's grace as you consider the effects of your actions on your life, the personal implications of what has happened, and then respond with the appropriate movements of heart. Ignatius then advises that you have a dialogue with the "mystery of salvation," perhaps contemplating God's grace in the midst of who you really are. Then, reflecting on Christ crucified, you speak out your mind and heart to him. This dialogue may involve asking for consultation, a personal favor, or advice on how to handle a difficult situation.[66] It may be as simple as asking for God's grace to guide you in the direction you should follow or for the right words to say in resolving a personal conflict.

In twelve-step terms, this type of reflection might mean asking for guidance in a specific situation. For example, if you neglected your spouse because you were busy pursuing your addiction, an apology would obviously be in order. The *Big Book* advises that "in meditation, we ask God what we should do about each specific matter. The right answer will come, if we want it."[67]

You might look at where spiritual consolation and desolation are occurring in your life and where your attitudes come from. To what ends do they lead you?[68] If they do not lead you to God, then perhaps you need to let go of some of them, or at least move on from them.

I continually need to watch out for distractions that cause me to avoid what is going on in my heart and often lead to desolation. For me, these distractions can be as simple as engaging in gossip or cynicism. In Ignatian thinking, after you work to remove some of these distractions of your life, you are freer to talk with Jesus (or in twelve-step terms, with God or your higher power), and allow him to immerse his heart and mind in you. This is what often takes place in the second week of the Spiritual Exercises, which is often considered the most important week. In this week, you seek to immerse yourself in the mystery of Christ. In contemplating that mystery (or God or your higher power), Ignatius desires not just that you use your mind, will, and imagination but also that you contemplate the mystery of yourself in order to allow God to manage your life. This is a powerful spiritual experience, and it is developed by trusting and letting go. In a way, you are measuring your own life against the Paschal Mystery.

Whereas in Ignatius's understanding, you are seeking your role in the Paschal Mystery, the spiritual process of the life, suffering, death, and resurrection of Christ, who emptied himself to God. In twelve-step terms you are asking for God's grace to guide you in your life from now on and to not let your shortcomings drive you. Your shortcomings may always be there, but you do not have to live out of them.

As Ignatius says, you should ask God to let you know how best you might serve God.[69] So "while I continue to contemplate [Jesus'] life, let me begin to examine myself and ask to what state of life or to what kind of lifestyle is God . . . leading me?"[70] For example, you might respond, "Perhaps I am a workaholic and I need to seek more balance in my life."

In the second week of the Spiritual Exercises, you are also encouraged to meditate on the "two standards," or in contemporary terms, the "two leaders, two strategies." This is essentially gaining an awareness of good versus evil. Here, *evil* is our tendency to make ourselves the center of everything, rather than seeing God as the center. We ask for knowledge of how we may be subtly deceived in this regard and for help in guarding ourselves against this deceit.[71]

Ignatius is emphatic that you should know your own weaknesses. He also uses the analogy of a military general: if you know your own weaknesses, you know how you can be attacked.[72] The New Testament also wisely reminds us: "Beloved, do not believe every spirit, but test the spirits to see whether they are from God; for many false prophets have gone out into the world" (1 John 4:1).

It is also wise to remember that any desolation you may feel when doing Step 5 may be a means of purifying and deepening your love for God, of preparing you for something new. Step 5 plays a crucial role in spiritual growth. John Cassian, the fourth-century ascetic who was inspired by the monks of Egypt and later introduced their wisdom to the West, talks about how compunction, which produces movements of the heart in the hidden recesses of the spirit, can later emerge as unspeakable joy.[73]

The consolation of tears (which Ignatius also speaks of) can also occur while completing Step 5:

> Sometimes the soul lies low, hidden in the depths of silence . . . with unspeakable groanings it pours out its longings to God. And sometimes it fills us with such sorrow and grief that it can only shake it off by melting into tears.[74]

Hopefully, when you complete a Step 5 you sense a shift of some sort. I found that during Ignatius's Spiritual Exercises I gained a greater understanding of my gifts and weaknesses, as well as of the need to let go of self in order for creativity and spirituality to shine and grow. I gained a great sense of being loved by God.

Humility is an integral part of the spiritual life, and it is important to define it. Humility is not allowing yourself to be exploited. Rather, it is about honesty, about discussing yourself and holding back nothing.[75] Only after telling the truth of your life and acknowledging your weaknesses and vulnerabilities—rather than letting egotistical concerns about what others might think drive you—can you make progress. In the AA tradition, humility "amounts to a clear recognition of what and who we really are, followed by a sincere attempt to become what we could be."[76]

Just as you must have humility and be able to empty yourself in order to face who you really are, realizing this is also a step on the journey toward God. The false self gradually gives way to the true self, which is hiding. Another of the desert fathers, St. John of Egypt, talks about this selfish, false, and illusory self that you can mistake for your real self. A priority in discerning this false self is to pray to God, "so that standing before God who is darkness [unknowable] the false self may be stripped away and the true image and likeness of God within be revealed."[77]

To start to find this true self, you need to follow the advice of another saint: Benedict suggested, "Listen . . . with the ear of your heart."[78] One of the Benedictine vows is for continual conversion of life, a conversion to a way of seeing. As the blind men plead in the Gospel stories, "Lord, Let me see again" (Mark 10:51) and "Lord, let our eyes be opened" (Matthew 20:33).

This—letting go of your old way of life and embracing the new through the action of God—is part of your continual call for conversion. Your *conversatio*, or your conversion and turning toward God, is an ongoing process in which you also aim for *metanoia*, a Greek word meaning "conversion of mind and heart."

Before you complete Step 5, you may feel alienated from your own center. Your self-centeredness may have caused you to do many wrong things, or at the very least it may have caused you unhappiness. Conversion helps free you from this darkness and leads you to becoming more other-centered. This, in a sense, is how we can understand the Catholic sacrament of penance. You move from a place of being fixated on self to a place of being fixated on the other: God, Jesus Christ, or a higher power. Discovering your center in God is true conversion, and it reconnects you to your own true center. As the Beatitudes say, "Blessed are the pure in heart, for they will see God" (Matthew 5:8).

Benedictine John Main, an expert on Christian meditation, expresses this as follows: "Our center is in God. To love God is to have our center of consciousness in him. Just as his love for us is manifested in the Incarnation by which he, by emptying himself, placed his center in us."[79]

With Step 5 you explore the responses of your heart. You look at where your heart is divided, where freedom and nonfreedom operate. The word of God (which means the Spirit of Christ in our hearts, in

Scripture, and in the Holy Spirit acting in the world) judges the movements and secret intentions of the heart:

> The word of God is living and active, sharper than any two-edged sword, piercing until it divides soul from spirit, joints from marrow; it is able to judge the thoughts and intentions of the heart. And before him no creature is hidden, but all are naked and laid bare to the eyes of the one to whom we must render an account. (Hebrews 4:12–13)

Self-knowledge is crucial on a twelve-step journey. It is also a way to compensate against desolation. In order to be free, you need not only to know who you are but also to desire to be known intimately by God. This knowledge only comes partially, and slowly. As we see in Paul's letter to the Corinthians (13:12): "Now we see in a mirror, dimly, but then we will see face-to-face. Now I know only in part; then I will know fully, even as I have been fully known."

A resolute change of heart and a resolve to allow God to manage your life is the potentiality that resides in Step 5. The reparation of wrongs comes in a later step, but at this point, it may be appropriate to simply know that you are forgiven by God, to be more willing to forgive those who have wronged you, and to be more willing to forgive yourself. This latter gift is most important.

The story of the prodigal son (Luke 15:11–32) in the New Testament also has an important message. The wayward son was received lovingly back into his father's home, after years of running up debts and living the high life. This caused his hardworking brother much envy and chagrin. The unconditional love and forgiveness of the father for the wayward son who returned home is similar to the unconditional love of God for us. God's love is given freely, regardless of anything we may have done. What matters most is that you are honest with God about who you really are.

What can occur after completing Step 5? The twelfth-century Cistercian monk Bernard of Clairvaux (Cistercians were a reformed group of Benedictines) noted that a spiritual journey involves listening to what is in our hearts:

> Only by the movement of my heart . . .
> did I recognize His presence . . .
> and I came to wonder
> at the depth of his wisdom.[80]

Julian of Norwich, a fourteenth-century nun who lived as an anchoress attached to a church in Norwich, England, left us with many beautiful and uplifting spiritual writings. In her day, she also gave solace to those who passed by her cell, often dispensing insightful spiritual guidance. Her message is clear: self-knowledge can open you up to God:

> We can never come to the full knowledge of God until we first clearly know our own soul. For until the time that it is in its full powers, we cannot be all holy. . . . Our passing life that we have here does not know in our senses what our self is, but we know in our faith. And when we know and see, truly and clearly, what our self is, then we shall know truly and clearly see and know our Lord God in the fullness of joy.[81]

6

Openness

Step 6: [We] were entirely ready to have God remove all these defects of character.

We must know that God regards our purity of heart and tears of compunction, not our many words.

—St. Benedict[82]

My Story: What Falls Away

By far, late 2008 until late 2009 was without doubt the worst year of my life. I can still remember how I put faith on the back doorstep one night. It was a February day when the worst bush fires had occurred in Victoria—Black Saturday they called it. It was my Black Saturday, too.

Five months earlier I had buried my lover of the previous three years, and two months later, my Jesuit spiritual director of the previous thirteen years. The two most significant men in my life, both of whom I had loved deeply, had gone. It was not an easy time. My boyfriend drowned tragically, becoming tangled in ropes one dark, stormy night—a metaphor for his life—and his funeral traumatized me.

That Saturday I had gotten into a minor altercation with a neighbor. We had bumped into each other's cars, and an argument ensued via email. The situation was compounded by the fact that I was already facing a potential legal battle with my apartment block. All was not well. I feared I would not be able to sell my property, and I felt angry and overwhelmed. I had no defenses against my feeling of rage, and I was besieged by an enormous well of grief from within. I felt I had no strength to fight anything.

I was in so much pain. The only place of safety I could envision for myself that day was a movie theater. So I went to see the Clint Eastwood–directed movie *The Changeling*, with Angelina Jolie as the protagonist fighting the forces of evil in a 1930s police force in an attempt to locate her missing son—who, it transpired, might have been brutally murdered. Not the best film to see when you are feeling down and oppressed by forces outside your control. What the movie did, however, was unleash a torrent of emotion—an extraordinary amount of grief that came up from inside me and exploded with a vengeance as I drove home from the cinema.

Yes, I had reason to feel sorry for myself. I remember that night saying to God, "Well, if this is the best you can do—then f**k you!" Yes, I had put God on the back burner—or banned him to the back porch. But I did this not entirely without faith. I knew that deep inside me I had a dark journey to complete, and I had to go through it before I could reach the light at the end of the tunnel. Unbeknownst to myself, grief had made me "entirely ready to have God remove all these defects of character," and I had a lot more letting go to do.

Discernment and Healing

Steps 6 and 7 enable you to address all in your experience that advances or hinders the soul in its quest for God. Both steps center on humility: being "entirely ready" and humble in spirit to allow God to remove whatever separates you from God. A key issue in both steps is willingness, and it requires humility and honesty. It's not for nothing that a twelve-step program catchphrase is "Honesty, open-mindedness, and willingness."

As Bill W. once wrote:

Let us never fear needed change . . .
The essence of all growth is a willingness
to change for the better and then an unremitting
willingness to shoulder whatever responsibility this entails.[83]

In Step 6 you need to be willing to let go of past fears and hurts. It is important to remember that you are moving toward wholeness, not perfection. Letting go also aids you in forgiveness. For example, along with self-centeredness, an inability to forgive yourself or believing that you are a failure, instead of a divine creation by God, may be a defect of character.

However earnestly you embark on this process in Step 6, you may never remove some of your unhealthy character traits. They may only lessen in their intensity and capacity to overpower you. So be sure to acknowledge your attributes as well as your faults.

During that time, 2009 and 2010, when I walked away from my house, my job, and material security, I was willing to have removed from my life the inessential things, both material and emotional. I lived like a gypsy for several months. I stripped my life down to the raw essentials. I was forced to gradually let go of the hurtful aspects of my past and move forward into the unknown, with nothing but my writing and a few small mustard seeds of remaining faith to sustain me.

The Franciscan spiritual writer Richard Rohr observes that there are three major things that undermine spirituality: the desire for power, prestige, and position. Often these things may have driven your life before, but seeking them caused enormous distress. As the popular poem "Desiderata" says, always there are lesser and greater persons than yourself.

There is a paradox we face with these powerful character traits. Some of them may in fact be caused by "wounds" and we may never get rid of them—we may just see them in a new light, or partially heal. Some of these wounds may stay with us but no longer dominate us to the same degree. This is part of the nature of a healing journey: learning to live with and accept some of our inherent flaws.

Much of the baggage we carry is connected to sacred wounds, according to Rohr. Such wounds may be our natural responses to the abusive behavior of other people. They may involve parents or other significant relationships, perhaps the legacy of severe emotional, sexual, or physical abuse. For many of us a combination of character traits we are born with and our social and familial environment causes us emotional damage.

You cannot fix these wounds yourself. Neither can you control your woundedness. Rather, it is what you do with those wounds, how you grow beyond them, incorporating them in yourself but not continuing to live out of them, that affects your spiritual growth.

Realizing that your perceptions of your world may have been distorted, which you may experience during Steps 6 and 7, may also help you grow into a conscious choice for God, Christ, your higher power. A freedom gained when you start to rid yourself of baggage for God also involves integrating decisions, choices, prayer, and action. Many of those whom Christ healed embody this message. In particular, the Gospel stories of the blind seeing again reflect this integration. For example, Bartimaeus, acknowledging Jesus as Lord and Master, tells him, "Let me see again." And Jesus replies, "Go; your faith has made you well." Bartimaeus immediately "regained his sight and followed him on the way" (Mark 10:51–52). So it is with you. A readiness to allow God to remove what separates you from God can open up your sight to see what you need to let go of.

Another biblical story with this theme of being released or freed is the resurrection of Lazarus in John's Gospel. Partly a story about resurrection and the recognition of Jesus as the Son of God, it is also a story about being set free from the ties that bind. When Jesus calls for the dead man, Lazarus, to come out, Lazarus comes out of the tomb, his feet and hands bound. It is then that Jesus calls on the crowd to "unbind him, and let him go" free (John 11:43).

The story is another way of understanding the Christian concept of triumph over death. Lazarus is coming back from a place of spiritual death as well. In relating this to your own situation, ask yourself how you can respond to Jesus' calls to Lazarus, to "come out," to be unbound, to be set free. While acknowledging and understanding of hurt and anger can help free you, or can help you cut ties, perhaps God is calling you back from the places where you don't belong, from those things that keep you in a state of "death."

When you undertake Steps 6 and 7, you desire that God set you free, that God unbind you from the things that hold you back. Again, in these steps, the emphasis is on desire and willingness, an intention, not simply action.

As in the previous steps, you must undergo this process at your own pace and in the ways you can. Some of your faults may be hard to let go of, and others you may never relinquish completely, such as egoism and fear.

I find fear the most difficult and entrenched characteristic, and equate it with a powerful state of desolation. Fear is a stifling emotion that can dramatically distort your perceptions of the world.

If you are "entirely ready" to embark on Step 6, you may desire deeper reflection. If you want to address Step 6 in a more intense way, then St. Ignatius offers powerful tools of prayer and reflection for discernment and decision making.

Discernment, thinking about what is going to lead you to become more in line with your true values, is crucial in this step, for your choices affect your spiritual life. Growing in an understanding of what your issues and others' issues are leads to awareness of what you need to let go of and strive toward. Becoming willing for God to remove your defects of character or traits that have held you back in life means being discerning about what you may need to change. This requires openness and receptiveness to the movements of your heart; it means asking which ones are from God and which are not from God.

You can begin Step 6 simply by saying a preparatory prayer from the first week of the Ignatian exercises. In your prayer, ask God for the grace that all your daily life, intentions, and actions be fully oriented toward the worship and service of God.

In this step, you are dealing with the movements of your heart, the movements of your soul that affect your interior life. Sometimes these movements may be a blatant move away from God; at other times, they may be subtler. In helping discern these movements, you need to ask which aspects of your nature lead to consolation—in other words, to an openness and love of God—and which lead to a move away from God, to desolation or darkness of your soul.[84]

"Good" and "evil" spirits come from within your very self, from outside of you, or from others.[85] "Evil spirits" in this context can be considered those subtle things that undermine your self-worth, that tell you that you are unlovable or a failure. They are those movements of heart and spirit that seek to separate you from your dependence on God or a higher power.

For those undergoing the "soul cleansing" that happens in Steps 6 and 7, it is helpful to think of Ignatius's words: "It is the way of the evil spirit to bite, sadden and put obstacles, disquieting with false reasons that one may not go on." In contrast, consolations bring a greater sense of courage and strength.[86] At this point you need to gradually develop discernment, for you may experience a mixture of these feelings as you undergo Steps 6 and 7.

I found in the reconciliation examen that when we notice God more in creation, the agitations, the remembrance of past hurts in relationships, came and went while the Good Spirit brought courage, consolation, and greater inspiration. I continually needed to remember the benefits I had received thus far, especially the sense of being loved and healed by God.

To embrace the will of God is to enter fully into the human experience, into Jesus' life, his desire, love, suffering, and feelings of abandonment. This is akin to experiencing the passion of Jesus Christ, as depicted in the third week of the Ignatian exercises. Feelings of compassion or distress may accompany this process, because you are dealing with powerful aspects of your humanity that have driven your life.[87]

Remember, there is a resurrection. In the fourth week of the Spiritual Exercises, God utterly consoles the soul and fills it with joy and light. After his troubles with the powers of the day, Jesus could have chosen the easier way, escaping into the desert. Rather, he chose to go back to Jerusalem and face his inevitable horrific crucifixion. The biggest temptation for Jesus, and for most of us, probably is to return to the safe and the familiar. We are often tempted to stay with the character traits that keep us bound up in the old behaviors that no longer serve us.

In Step 6 you look with humility and discernment at those characteristics that may have caused you immense pain and hardship in your life. You recognize that they are still with you and acknowledge your readiness to let them go—to let go of what was once part of you, what was once a familiar way of being.

7

The New Self Begins to Emerge

Step 7: [We] humbly asked Him to remove our shortcomings.

O Lord, you were turning me around to look at myself. For I had placed myself behind my own back, refusing to see myself. . . . [Y]ou brought me face to face with myself once more.

—St. Augustine[88]

My Story: Moving On

Grief is like a tsunami. It contains so many things. There is not a lot that is pleasant about grief. When we feel grief, we have no time for niceties or people pleasing. But one positive thing that stems from grief is that it frees us from inessential things, because when we grieve, we pare life down to only the things that matter.

It took me a year to get through the worst of my grief after experiencing such loss, and by November 2009 I had left behind an apartment I had owned and lived in for thirteen years and a job I had held for nine years (and that had been wearing me thin for a long time), I had severed a thirty-five year friendship that had become toxic, I had paid off all my debts, and I had walked away from my previous life. A purgation, yes, but grief can do that. It can strip away all that is not essential and leave us with the bare bones of emotion and a few pure fragments of what constitutes our essential unmitigated self.

It was only when I drove away from that place and embarked on a road trip by myself along Australia's Great Ocean Road on the

Victorian coastline (one of the most beautiful places in the world) that I realized I was symbolically shedding parts of my former life along the way. As I drove down the curved road and heard the sounds of the wild southern Indian Ocean, I felt I was leaving behind the parts of my life, of myself, that no longer served me. The trauma of my losses forced me to release them.

Releasing What No Longer Works

The nature of Step 7 is that you have come to a point at which you humbly ask God to free you from specific character faults or obsessive attachments that separate you from spiritual and inner freedom. This is a continual lifelong process, so you may, as I did, find yourself coming back to this step regularly.

While pain may have been the price you paid to eventually reach this insight, the blessing has been a measure of humility. Humility, when honest, can release tension and as you'll soon discover, can heal your pain.[89]

Recognizing your own frailties enables you to move out from yourself, to begin to let go of self, to become more Other focused and closer to God and to the reality of yourself. You come to not fear pain so much but to desire humility as an integral part of your spiritual growth.

On beginning Step 7, if you are still clinging to something and cannot let go, you might ask God to help you be willing. When ready, say something like this:

My Creator, I am now willing that you should have all of me, good and bad. I pray that you now remove from me every single defect of character, which stands in the way of my usefulness to you and my fellows. Grant me strength, as I go out from here, to do your bidding. Amen.[90]

Step 7 builds on the moral inventory in previous steps, in that it reminds us that some aspects of our humanity, when they seek to dominate us, can become things that hold us back. These things include pride, fear, shame, and lust. Pride, in particular, is a big one: it can stifle your willingness to reach out to God or others.

Because Step 7 is taken in humility, it can help you let go of false pride, which deludes you into thinking that you must stay in control and not let others know what is going on in your heart. Yet owning up to your flaws can turn them into assets. You can learn and grow from them. Your failures and vulnerabilities can become tools of inner knowledge with which you can help both yourself and others. Strength can come out of weakness, humility is strength, and as it says in the Gospels: "The last will be first, and the first will be last" (Matthew 20:16), "Those who find their life will lose it, and those who lose their life for my sake will find it" (Matthew 10:39), and "The least among all of you is the greatest" (Luke 9:48).

A great message for those who are on a spiritual path is to not perceive yourself as conquering your shortcomings, but rather to accept that only God has the capacity to relieve your burdens. Such acceptance puts you in a position of great spiritual fortitude. Also, by the very path you choose, you are in a sense countercultural: you no longer worship the illusion of personal power, which you know from experience has brought you destruction in one form or another or is, at the very least, finite.

It is also important to remember that asking God to remove your shortcomings may also mean that they will be removed in God's time frame, not yours, and that some of those shortcomings may never be removed from your life.

Acknowledging that you are truly human and are doing your best can help you complete Step 7. Because you are human, you need to accept that you will probably take many character flaws with you to the grave.

Understanding that, ultimately, you know nothing is another key to spiritual wisdom. Step 7 may involve trusting in God to reveal what you need to let go of, as well as what you may have to live with as part of your own woundedness. That sacred wound may indeed be transformed into an asset. The monk John Cassian advised:

> For he is next door to understanding
> who carefully recognizes
> what he ought to ask about,
> nor is he far from knowledge
> who begins to understand how ignorant he is.[91]

Similar to Step 7, the point of the Ignatian Spiritual Exercises is to grow in freedom and to attend to the movement of God's spirit in you. The attainment of true spiritual freedom, according to Ignatius, comes about by bringing an order of values into your life. Out of that order of values you can make choices and decisions free of influence from any obsessive attachment.

When my experience of grief and trauma in my "purgation decade" of 2000–2009 forced me to reevaluate what really mattered to me, I let go of obsessive materialism and unhealthy emotional attachments, such as professional status. Instead, I found my genesis as a writer and came to focus on my other gifts as a chaplain and educator. I let go of those things that no longer served me.

Often, we focus on everything else in our life except that one thing we most need to do, open our heart to God. We may pray or work even harder than usual rather than facing a particular attachment.[92] It is in such circumstances that you may find that you need to humbly ask for God to remove your shortcomings. Doing so can help you diffuse or let go of an attachment. For example, you may have a way of avoiding looking at your own fears and resentments in a relationship by obsessively helping others. In the guise of this good act, you may actually be doing yourself harm, and failing to attend to the needs of your closest relationships.

Fear of failure can also stop you from growing as a person. You might ask yourself, "Where have I missed the mark in my own life? Where did I miss opportunities for growth or self-fulfillment because of my own nature? How can I overcome this?"

St. Augustine, the bishop of Hippo (in today's Algeria) in the fourth century, struggled with many of these same questions and difficulties in his famous pilgrimage of conversion. Augustine's spirituality was a "mysticism of action." He saw no conflict between a life of contemplation and a life of action. He sought intimacy with God, but he also lived very much in the world. A person who experienced a gradual journey of conversion after many years of being a womanizer and pleasure seeker, Augustine believed that conversion to faith comes about through God's grace. We allow for an openness to grace, which is a gift, and then all the joys that come into our life come from God.

Augustine's story is testimony to the fact that there is no greater miracle than faith and the inner transformation brought about by owning up to who you really are.

Augustine's famous treatise *Confessions* captures the emotional, passionate, and moving encounter between the human soul that hungers for intimacy with God and the flawed human condition, which manifests as a conflict between "Truth" and the life of habit, inner conflict and worldly pursuits, and a struggle with intention.

These ideas are applicable to the practice of Step 7. Much of what Augustine struggled with concerned the conflict between God's will and what we might call self-will today: the struggle with human nature, on the one hand, and the call to be with God, on the other.

Augustine believed that he was bound by the chains of his obsessions and compulsions. His conversion was slow yet intense. It may be difficult today to identify with Augustine's struggle to renounce his relationships with women (and yes, what might seem extremism and misogyny), but as you come back to Step 7 regularly, you might begin to see his story in relation to the shortcomings that dominate your own life. Asking God to remove the emptiness that you often encounter when you look for satisfaction in material things outside of yourself is just one example of this.

Feelings of occasional despair, frustration, or distance from God are inevitable stumbling blocks in a serious spiritual journey. Augustine desired spiritual fulfillment but feared it might mean losing what was familiar and comfortable to him.

He knew only too well, though, that we often struggle with our intentions and can deceive ourselves with our own motives. Augustine reminds us:

> The appearance of what we do
> is often different from the intention
> with which we do it,
> and the circumstances at the time may not be clear.[93]

All of your experiences, both good and bad, can teach you something. Despite his mystical experiences and epiphanies along the way, Augustine all too readily fell back into his old behavior. It took time before he was fully converted. Yet these experiences did not leave him untouched by the presence of God.

It is no surprise that Augustine, who would have been familiar with the life of the desert monk St. Anthony of Egypt, eventually came to understand that it is in the innermost call of your heart that you can listen to and ultimately find God:

> O God, hope of my youth, where were you all this time? Where were you hiding from me. . . . Yet I was walking on a treacherous path, in darkness. I was looking for you outside myself, and I did not find the God of my own heart.[94]

Augustine's struggles ultimately brought him face-to-face with his own fragility. This is also your task in this step: to be naked before your true self and your conscience. Augustine also found out through his own searching that many of our learned behaviors are hard to relinquish:

> While Truth teaches [the soul] to prefer one course, habit prevents it from relinquishing the other. . . . [T]his was the nature of my sickness. I was in torment. . . . And you, O lord, never ceased to watch over my secret heart.[95]

Like many of the desert fathers and mothers, Augustine's eventual conversion brought him the gift of tears:

> I probed the hidden depths of my soul and
> wrung its pitiful secrets from it,
> and when I mustered them all before the eyes of my heart,
> a great storm broke within me,
> bringing with it a great deluge of tears.[96]

When you are completing the steps of taking a moral inventory, Augustine's contribution to your progress may well be his understanding of the role of God's grace and mercy in a person's life:

> Where else, then, did I find you, to learn of you, unless it was in yourself, above me? Whether we approach you or depart from you, you are not confined in any place. You are Truth, and you are everywhere present where all seek counsel of you. . . . The [one] who serves you best is the one who is less intent on hearing from you what he wills to hear than on shaping his will according to what he hears from you.[97]

Augustine knew that, despite the uncertainty we face on a spiritual journey, "the only firm promise we have is [God's] mercy."[98] So, "cast yourself upon God and have no fear."[99]

8

Owning Up to the Past

Step 8: [We] made a list of all persons we had harmed, and became willing to make amends to them all.

Some wrongs we can never fully right.

—*Alcoholics Anonymous*[100]

My Story: Making Amends

I have often had to make amends over the years, and one person on that list was my sister. With her it was a difficult amends to make, since I did not see her much before her death in 1993. Our childhoods and teenage years were fraught with tension and difficulties, and we often clashed because of our volatile temperaments and family environment. Her intellectual and mental health disabilities had always caused me angst growing up, and as sad as I am to admit it, I sometimes felt shame about her behavior. My own behavior, of course, was far from exemplary, and I realize that both of us were victims of our own particular type of prison. I lashed out at her sometimes and was unavailable as a sister. Later, when she probably needed me as an adult, we both lived in different states and had become estranged.

About five years after her death, after I had met my spiritual mentor Brian Stoney and his community of people living on the street, I gained an understanding of why we sometimes lash out at vulnerable people who are also damaged. They trigger us, and they show us our own flaws to our face.

After I gained that understanding, when I would confront a woman who reminded me of my sister—loud, damaged, and often socially inappropriate—I would feel compassion and show some small act of kindness. That was my living amends. I was also able to pray my amends to my sister and ask for her forgiveness.

Breaking the Ties That Bind

All of us forgive in different ways and have different types of wounds that we carry with us. But forgiveness is about becoming free of the wounds we hold on to. Forgiveness can bless us with freedom and distance from a situation that may have troubled us for a long time, not to mention long-yearned-for relief and peace of mind.

Steps 8 and 9 are about looking at all areas of your life, your relationships in particular, and becoming willing to set things right, to make amends to people you have harmed. They aim to repair past wrongs and free yourself of guilt so that you can live in peace. Then you are free to become more connected to yourself and to other people.

To start to make amends may mean being willing to undertake a gentle exercise in reparation for something you have done or a token act of penance, such as a symbolic intention to become more willing to change your behavior from here on out. Or it may involve making a generous gesture toward someone you have harmed or an apology along with a humble and honest explanation for your past behavior. Remember the words often attributed to Mahatma Gandhi: "be the change you wish to see in the world." There is no greater demonstration of true amends than your action, your presence as a better, more loving human being.

You may never do all the steps fully, but what matters is that you do them to the best of your ability as issues arise for you. There may be some wrongs that you can never right, but this is where acceptance comes in. Above all, you need to forgive yourself. That is often the hardest part.

One way to start is by making a list of the people, debts, or situations that are obvious priorities for reparation. This is the way you begin to "straighten out the past." As with the other steps, you may come back to Steps 8 and 9 regularly—your willingness to do so is always what counts.

Remember that you are experiencing a "death" of self in these steps, so you need to pray for direction. In regard to your attitudes toward those who have harmed you, it is also wise to practice prayerful discernment and perhaps seek spiritual guidance. Prayer is not only a way you can forgive; it is also a way of discerning where you need to practice forgiveness.

If you are unsure, you can also ask God to direct you to those people to whom you should make amends. You may not be able to locate all whom you have harmed, or even remember whom you have harmed in your life, but you can pray for the willingness to make amends where appropriate. Some of the Ignatian tools of discernment or prayerful reflection may also be helpful here.[101]

To avoid getting caught up in over scrupulous or unnecessary guilt, it is wise to listen to your heart. It has the answer. As Scripture tells us: "It is not good to feel shame in every circumstance, nor is every kind of abashment to be approved" (Ecclesiastes 41:16). Because God alone reads our hearts, we are likely to be judged not by our acts but by our intentions.

When you start working on owning up to your past in Steps 8 and 9, humility, poverty of spirit—emptying oneself through humility and openness so that one can receive God's grace—and a willingness to be led where you need to go will guide you. All you can do is trust.

9
Making Up for the Past

Step 9: [We] made direct amends to such people wherever possible except when to do so would injure them or others.

The Lord waits for us daily to translate into action, as we should, his holy teachings. Therefore our life span has been lengthened by way of a truce, that we may amend our misdeeds.

—St. Benedict[102]

Carol's Story

"The twelve steps for me are a way to God and freedom. They are my lifeline, my backbone. It's two o'clock in the morning, and I arrive at the Alcoholics Anonymous Central Office in Los Angeles, California. I am on a faith journey to the United States, practicing Step 3—abandoning myself to God. It is my fourth sober birthday, and I want to welcome the day in gratitude. So I offer to answer the phones in the early hours of this Friday morning. I get three calls; I talk to one woman for forty minutes. It's her second day of sobriety—she can't sleep, and she's killing time before an early-morning meeting.

"I notice an amends letter to my brother poking out of my journal. I had no intention of bringing it, and all of a sudden I am dialing his number in Australia. It's Friday night, and he's home, and I find myself asking him if it is a good time, if he is willing to listen to an amends letter I have written to him. I explain it's part of my program and he says, 'Of course.'

"I read him the letter, word for word. At the time I wrote it, I had no intention of actually reading it to him. I finish and wait. And he thanks me and says how beautiful it is, and that he is touched, and that it is the best thing that has happened to him all week.

"After I hang up the phone, I sit back in my chair, look around the office. At that moment, gratitude fills my soul and every cell in my body. Sometimes there are not enough words for it. A warm feeling washes over me and through me. I feel incredibly close to God.

"Step 9 is my first major experience that the steps are working in my life. I am a long way from the terrified, insane, drug-and-alcohol-dependent girl who crawled into these rooms. I say a prayer of thanks: to God, for my sobriety, for my life, and for the relationship I have been given with my brother."

Reaching Out in a New Way

Much of the work of Step 9 involves further letting go of the ego, turning away from yourself to look out on the world. As Carol's story shows, it is very much about facing the things you have done or have failed to do and about being accountable. Again, your humility is your strength.

Reconciliation (formerly called confession) is the traditional sacrament of penance in the Catholic Church. Many people undergo this sacramental rite because they intuitively know that "the truth will set them free."

The idea of penance in the history of Christianity was to make reparations for one's past moral failures. Today, we might perceive it as feeling deep sorrow for what we have done.[103] It also means having a firm desire to make things right, to make amends, and to devote ourselves more readily to God.[104] We desire to make up for what we have done, and we accept whatever consequences come with that intention.

Remember Jesus' words: "I have come to call not the righteous but sinners to repentance" (Luke 5:32).

The act of reconciliation is a sacramental encounter that bestows on us the knowledge that Christ is truly present.[105] The Benedictine John Main writes:

> Every sacramental reality
> is a celebration of the reality of the presence of Christ
> united to our human spirit,
> praying to the Father in our human heart.[106]

This sacramental reality can be a healing act and bonding act; it can lead you to greater intimacy with God. Reconciliation can free you up to be more open to love and to be more forgiving of others. The same applies to the act of making amends. In whatever form it takes, making amends can be viewed as a loving response to God's movements in your heart. In Steps 8 and 9, we attempt to do this to the best of our ability.

In the pre-Christian biblical tradition, a year of jubilee was a time when debts were wiped away, slaves freed, and alienated land returned to its ancestral owners. In the book of Leviticus, God speaks to Moses on Mt. Sinai, instructing him about the year of jubilee, telling him:

> [It will be] a jubilee for you: you shall return, every one of you, to your property and everyone of you to your family. . . . When you make a sale to your neighbor or buy from your neighbor, you shall not cheat one another. . . . [F]or I am the LORD your God. (Leviticus 25:11–17)

A jubilee year occurred every fifty years; the idea was to liberate the oppressed and bring about atonement and redemption. It would begin on Yom Kippur, the Day of Atonement, a Jewish fast day during which the community ritually atoned for its sins. Symbolically and actively, the day is a time for reconciliation, a time to make things right.

This same principle of the jubilee year and atonement applies to the idea of reconciliation on your own spiritual journey. You can reconcile by making things right, by becoming willing to clear away "debts" where you have incurred them and attempting to repair damaged relationships.

Prayer is a journey to the center of your being, and it has the power to release you from the burden of self-obsession and bring you closer to God. Once you are more connected to the Other, whether through prayer, ritual, sacrament, or sharing your stories, you can reconnect with other people. Compassion for self will then lead to compassion for others.

The true purpose of religion should be to reconnect people with the Other. The Latin root of *religion* suggests a relinking or reconnection.[107] The Franciscan Richard Rohr observed that all great religion, all healthy religion, is about what you do with your pain—how you transform it and come out on the other side resurrected.[108] Step 9 involves this too. John Main writes:

> The Lord, as we know, purifies those who draw near to him
> in a growing consciousness of his supreme reality.
> The roots of our egoism are dried up by the work of love that
>   is our prayer.
> And as we turn more openly to the Spirit, in our inmost being,
> so does the phantom of the ego gradually disappear.[109]

Humility deepens and nurtures the spiritual life, yet it is often overtaken by the ego. Thus, driving the twelve steps, and Step 9 in particular, are humility and charity. To quote one of the desert fathers:

> If you see [someone] pure and humble,
> that is a great vision.
> For what is greater than such a vision,
> to see the invisible God in a visible [person].[110]

God means for you to experience all of your humanity, including your own woundedness. As the beaten down know only too well, those who open themselves to God, through emptiness and poverty of spirit—being completely open for God—can sometimes experience God more intensely.

St. Benedict also knew that poverty of spirit is the pathway to God and freedom. It brings us life. For those who need to make amends, although your past behavior may have held you back, caused you and others harm, or brought you "death," you now can move into "life": "Do you not realize that God's kindness is meant to lead you to repent?" (Romans 2:4).

And indeed the Lord assures us in his love: "I have no pleasure in the death of the wicked, but that the wicked turn from their ways and live" (Ezekiel 33:11).[111]

When you face another human being and make amends, whether or not that person forgives you, you can encounter the presence of God.

When I lit candles and said prayers and made amends with people who had died, like my sister and my former boyfriend, I got a sense of peace. I was truly honest and myself in that moment, without expectations.

The poverty of spirit, the openness to God's grace without expectations that the mystics embody is, in a way, what we aim for in the spiritual life. Poverty of spirit, which we often experience through our own flaws, becomes an asset. For many of us, it may have been what led us to God. Bill W. knew this only too well in relation to his experience of alcoholism:

> So it is necessary for all of us to accept whatever positive gifts we receive with a deep humility, always bearing in mind that our negative attitudes were first necessary as a means of reducing us to such a state that we would be ready for a gift of the positive ones via the conversion experience. Your own alcoholism and the immense

deflation that finally resulted are indeed the foundation upon which your spiritual experience rests.[112]

Step 9 can bring about a great feeling of gratitude and can make you feel closer to God. It can also bring about a feeling of being forgiven and a real sense of letting go of the past and the all-pervading sense of alienation and abandonment.

10

Continual Transformation

Step 10: [We] continued to take personal inventory and when we were wrong promptly admitted it.

O LORD, you have searched me and known me.

—Psalm 139

Jane's Story

"It is sometimes difficult to take responsibility for, or even be able to see with any clarity, what has actually occurred in an unpleasant situation. It is much easier to take the high moral ground and blame the other. However, sometimes special spiritual friends can inspire great gifts to come from otherwise dark situations. I was lucky to have such a friend. His name was Bill.

"My early recovery from active alcoholism was a bewildering and fearful time. Every area of my life was in tatters. I heard a saying once that 'life lived as a means to an end is self-robbery.' I was bankrupt in all areas of my life.

"It was suggested to me that as soon as I was physically well, I get a job to support my son and pay off the debts I had. I was also looking after my grandfather. Although it was very tiring, I started to feel better about myself. Then Grandfather died, and this left me lonely and quite bereft. Two years later my mother died, and my grief compounded. However, it did mean that I was quite well off financially, so I stopped work and started university.

"At this stage, a woman who appeared very consoling and helpful befriended me. After a while she suggested that I finance her in part ownership of a house. I later realized the old saying 'a fool and his money are soon parted.' The house went; the money went. On top of all that, my son's life was falling apart, and I was trying to finish an honors degree. My life was in chaos, and my heart was filled with resentment.

"When I talked with Bill I was extremely angry and self-righteous. He cut me short and said, 'If you want to learn anything from this experience, then ask yourself, Why was I there? What did I expect to gain from this situation?' He said that if I could see my own part in the situation, then I would find out how I had compromised myself subconsciously."

Growing in Self-Awareness

Step 10 is about bringing together all that you have learned in Steps 4–9 into your daily life. You can experience it with growing clarity, as Jane's story shows. By looking honestly at her part in being exploited, Jane was able to grow.

Allowing for the gradual healing of destructive and negative patterns is part of acceptance and adhering to the twelve-step philosophy of growing along spiritual lines rather than aiming for spiritual perfection. Praying for insight into why you do what you do, accepting it, and praying for it to be released from you is a start. Practicing forgiveness of self and others is also part of this process. God is always able to forgive, regardless of what we do wrong in life. The great stories of Scripture remind us of this forgiveness: the story of the prodigal son (Luke 15:11–32), the woman caught in adultery (John 8:1–11), the woman who wept over Jesus' feet at the house of Simon the Pharisee (Luke 7:36–50), the treatise to love your enemies (Luke 6:27–35).

As Jane's story demonstrates, to continue taking a personal moral inventory is not "giving yourself a hard time" or looking for defects. Rather, it is recognizing where certain behaviors interrupt the flow of your life or keep you separate from the knowledge that you are truly loved by God. This is an important point. The woman at Jesus' feet was forgiven because she had shown such great love (Luke 7:47).

Self-knowledge helps to liberate us. The core things that used to motivate and drive us, no longer dominate or control us to the same degree:

> We have entered the world of Spirit.
> Our next function is to grow in understanding and
>   effectiveness.
> This is not an overnight matter. It should continue for our
>   lifetime.
> Continue to watch for selfishness, dishonesty, resentment, and
>   fear.[113]

Happiness and contentment are often by-products of setting things right as you go along. The blessing of greater spiritual awareness gives you the ability to look at those things that bring you closer to God and those that distance you from God. You may also realize that much peace of mind comes from acceptance and gratitude. This is the key to Step 10:

> An honest regret for harms done, a genuine gratitude for blessings received, and a willingness to try for better things tomorrow will be the permanent assets we shall seek. . . . [H]aving searched our hearts with neither fear nor favor, we can truly thank God for the blessings we have received and sleep in good conscience.[114]

If you do not know what you need to take account of in your life, if you reach a roadblock, pray for guidance. Many of the Davidic psalms in the Old Testament can offer comfort. They reflect a passionate faith relationship with God amid the highs and lows of life, as well as the struggles implicit in an uncertain world. Attributed to David, they also show that despite his struggles, David eventually became king of Israel. The psalms might remind you that God has a plan for your life, even though that plan may be a mystery:

> How weighty to me are your thoughts, O God!
>   How vast is the sum of them!
> I try to count them—they are more than the sand;
>   I come to the end—I am still with you. . . .
>
> Search me, O God, and know my heart;
>   test me and know my thoughts.
> See if there is any wicked way in me,
>   and lead me in the way everlasting.
>
> —Psalm 139:17–24

Ignatian tools of discernment and decision making may be beneficial during Step 10, especially in discerning where consolation and desolation occur in your life.[115] The process can be about being aware and noticing the things that touch you, a reminder that "we see more clearly that the free gift of consolation is not something we can control, buy, or make our own."[116] Grace is a gift from God, not something of your own doing:

> Do not say to yourself, "My power and the might of my own hand have gained me this wealth." But remember the Lord your God, for it is he who gives you power to get wealth, so that he may confirm his covenant that he swore to your ancestors, as he is doing today. (Deuteronomy 8:17–18)

Ignatian spirituality emphasizes that if you know your own weaknesses, then you know how you can lose the way. This means that we should be aware of subtle impulses that are actually self-destructive. The "evil spirits" that St. Ignatius referred to are not necessarily evil in themselves; rather, they are emotions or drives that can lead us one way or another—away from God. Like a false lover, says Ignatius, the "evil spirit" knows your weaknesses and can capitalize on them.[117]

For example, Jane's situation might have revealed to her that she had an excessive need to be needed. Maybe when you begin to love someone and get close to that person you are fearful of rejection. Your low self-esteem embeds itself in you, telling you that you are worthless or don't deserve love, and so you sabotage the relationship. Such subtle feelings can in fact be destructive.

When I did the Spiritual Exercises I found I needed God to continually remind me to come back to the core of God's love and to remember that other people, places, and things might lead me into the web of the evil spirit. My feelings of anxiety often centered on anticipation about the future. So when I would do my awareness examen at the end of the day, I would pray for insight into greater truth and to be free from fear, confusion, anticipation, and uncertainty in order to let spirituality and creativity flow. So my examen, where I reflected on God's presence and direction in my day, revealed the necessity of me staying present to self, God, and the present moment, and not to be too fazed by distractions or irritations.

Despite its origins in a world of social chaos and political uncertainty—much like our own world today—the Rule of Benedict espoused the need to strive for balance in life. It did not advocate extreme asceticism, but it focused on the life of Christ within the individual. Much like the mystical writers, the rule emphasized singleness of heart in seeking only God and the spiritual bliss that comes through unceasing charity and prayer.

Seeking balance can be a path to inner harmony. When you are working toward a greater balance and acceptance in your life, you need to remind yourself that there are times when, despite your willingness, you cannot escape from entrenched, negative, self-destructive patterns of behavior that have long been a part of your psyche or personality.

Peeling away the onion layers, confronting fear and the obsession with self, can be a lifelong endeavor. Even though therapy can help, it takes a long time for the truth of the soul, our deepest essence as human beings, to make itself known.

You can think of what Christians traditionally know as "sin" or bad behavior as alienation from your center. Sin is really a disconnection or fragmentation from your loving self, from God. Benedictine John Main describes this as follows:

> Self-centeredness,
> being locked into one's self as a monad,
> and living the nightmare of finding only distorted images of
>   this illusion
> wherever one looks, and in whomsoever one meets.[118]

Continual conversion, or *metanoia* (the Greek word signifying radical change and conversion of heart), helps liberate and summon you from this state of disconnectedness or fragmentation by allowing you to be other-centered, which helps lead you to God. This means that you are continually keeping track or taking a personal inventory of the things that hold you back and prevent you from moving on to discover different aspects of your life.

In 1373, Julian of Norwich, a mystic and anchoress of great influence, experienced her "Showings." In these, she visually, emotionally, and spiritually witnessed the passion of Christ. Before her spiritual revelations, she prayed to experience the wounds of contrition, compassion, and longing for God.[119]

In her cell, adjoined to a church in Norwich, England, many people would come to her window to seek advice and spiritual guidance on all manner of problems. Her writings still remind us that God's love is present regardless of what we do and that sometimes, like Jane at the beginning of this chapter, we need to see certain things about ourselves. But it may take adversity to reveal them:

We need to fall, and we need to see it; for if we did not fall,
we should not know how feeble and how wretched we are in
  ourselves,
nor, too, should we know so completely the wonderful love of
  our Creator.[120]

Throughout her writings, Julian emphasizes the great insight that, although suffering and the adversity brought on by human behavior always occur in life, these states are temporary—ultimately, all will be well. Long after her famous visions of the passion of Christ had stopped, Julian offered these words to reassure those who continually fall into negative patterns that they need not despair:

Often I wondered why [in] the great foreseeing wisdom of God the beginning of sin was not letted. . . . And our Lord answered: "Sin is behovable [inevitable], but all shall be well, and all shall be well and all manner of things shall be well."[121]

You may suffer and get caught up in your faults, but doing so is temporary. Blessings can follow:

And it seems to me that this pain is something for a time,
    for it
purges us and makes us know ourselves and ask for mercy;
    for the
Passion of our Lord is comfort to us against all this, and that
    is his
blessed will for all who will be saved. He comforts readily and
sweetly with his words, and says: But all will be well, and
    every kind
of thing will be well.[122]

11

Continuing on the Journey

Step 11: [We] sought through prayer and meditation to improve our conscious contact with God as we understood Him, praying only for knowledge of His will for us and the power to carry that out.

> *But my friends should know truly*
> *That the more I draw them,*
> *The nearer they come to me.*
> *When [a person] makes a conquest over self,*
> *So that suffering and consolation weigh equally,*
> *Then will I raise him to blessedness*
> *And let him taste eternal life.*

—Mechthild of Magdeburg[123]

Therese's Story

"Practicing Step 11 is the key to a happy sobriety for me. It is a source of wisdom, a creative guide to right action and right thinking. It leads to a fuller, more abundant life—one not available without conscious contact with my higher power.

"In the early days of my recovery, I held rigidly onto the God I heard about in meetings, praying fervently for another day's sobriety every morning and thanking God for that sobriety at the end of the day. God was a force for intervention in my life at that time. I believed that God wanted change and total commitment from me. I would ask God to change this or that difficult situation, or this or that unacceptable thing in my personality.

"At some point, after a long period on my own, I came to believe that God wanted me to accept 'the hard thing'—entering the convent. I thought that this would prove my devotion. It was not what I wanted, but at the time I had a hard, albeit loving God—one not of desire but of demands. A wise sponsor had advised me to wait until I was five years sober before making that decision.

"When my recovery became more of an everyday thing, I began to realize that God was not what I had thought. Sobriety came to be less about 'being good' than about 'being real.' God did not always answer my prayers in the ways or times I asked. I entered a period of darkness in my prayer life that I found very hard to understand. I would pray earnestly for help with some defect, such as resentment or anger, and find that it did not go away. The interventionist God gave way to a God of mysterious absence. The old sureties failed, and my prayer life became dry and hard, like a desert walk to an unknown destination without a reliable guide.

"More recently, I have come back to a very simple form of prayer and meditation. Every morning, I spend between ten minutes and half an hour just making myself available to my higher power, breathing in and out and trying to let go of thoughts and embrace the presence of God. Sometimes I read a passage from the Bible, taken from church readings for the day. It is simple, but it is not easy. I now know what the Buddhists mean by the 'monkey mind'!

"Mostly, I just sit with my jumble and tumble of thoughts and try to bring my mind back to my breathing. While I rarely experience much serenity, I find that taking time to pray and meditate really makes a difference to my day. I often respond intuitively to difficult situations in ways I know would not have been available to me if I had not spent time with God in the morning. I see more beauty and more life around me. I am more open and relaxed with people.

"Nowadays, God is a mysterious presence in my life that enables me to accept those parts of myself I cannot change. While much of my own shadow side is still part of my life, the difference is that now it matters less. God is part of the chaos as well as the creativity in my life, the unconscious as well as the conscious. Step 11 has opened doors in my life I did not even dream were there."

God as Your Ally

As Therese's story reflects, prayer and meditation to a God or higher power of your own understanding enhance a sense of belonging and purposefulness. Praying for the power to carry out God's will can also help you accept that all will be well. It may result in your not getting so caught up in attachments or stressing over the small things.

Therese's story also emphasizes that there will be times in your life when you will revisit the desert experience, when your old self resurfaces or your faults temporarily take you over. That desert experience may come to you in the form of emptiness, depression, desolation, unhealthy behaviors, or simply a feeling of uncertainty or distance from God. It's important to remember that when you're experiencing trouble or distress, God is calling you closer.

As with Therese, moving through the twelve steps gives you the resources to deal with those desert experiences. You may also come to realize that Step 11 is as much about getting to know your real self as it is about coming to love and accept that reality. Since you know that suffering is part of life, you seek to maintain constant contact with God through prayer and meditation. You know that this is where peace and your freedom to "be" lies and where the answers will ultimately come.

St. Teresa of Ávila, a friend and protégé of spiritual director St. John of the Cross, advocated what she called "mental prayer," and she saw mutual love, detachment, and humility as the keystones of the spiritual life. For the down-to-earth Teresa, Jesus and God are friends, and mental prayer means "nothing else than an intimate sharing between friends; it means taking time frequently to be alone with Him who we know loves us."[124] You might apply this approach to Step 11, and it could take the form of writing, talking, and conversational praying, and so on.

In order to experience greater intimacy with God, you need to believe, hope, love, and know your own emptiness. Bearing this in mind, another intense and powerful form of prayer and meditation is the ancient wisdom of *lectio divina*, sometimes referred to as meditation, reading of the Word, or holy reading.

Meditation is part of all the great spiritual traditions. Put simply, it is about seeking to empty the mind and heart of distractions, being still, and allowing the Spirit to be present in you. There are many ways to meditate. Meditation usually takes the form of sitting on a chair, with feet flat, breathing deeply for a minimum of ten minutes but ideally for about half an hour.

For those unfamiliar with meditation, you can begin by simply setting aside twenty minutes in your day and repeating a mantra (a word or phrase) in your head, over and over again. A good mantra is the Aramaic (the ancient Hebrew Jesus spoke) *maranatha*, which means "Come, Lord, come." I find that is the best mantra for me, but you can use whatever mantra appeals to you, so long as it is simple. You can also sit in silence with quiet meditative music in the background (I like Gregorian chant). In meditation you do not fight the intrusive thoughts or feelings that come and go, but rather you accept them, let them go, and keep focusing on your mantra.

Lectio divina is profound, because it combines prayer and meditation. In prayer you speak to God, saying words of homage or asking for guidance; in meditation, you empty your mind of thoughts and continually recite a mantra of your choosing. Broken down into parts, this prayer method is as follows: *lectio, meditatio, oratio, contemplatio, evangelizatio, rumination,* or read, understand, reflect, pray, be still, respond, and continue to ponder.[125] In simpler terms, this involves reading a short spiritual text and "listening with the ear of your heart," understanding and reflecting on the text and considering how it might be applied in your life, then praying on your insights. Meditation using a mantra is often the easiest way to enter *lectio divina.*

You might think about what God is calling you to do and continue to think on a phrase from the text, or a message that has spoken to you, throughout the rest of the day. The message may be as simple as "Let go and let God." This entire prayer process of *lectio divina* may take at least half an hour, but this method of contemplation can be a powerful focus for your daily life, particularly for those times when you feel unsettled or stressed. It also sums up Step 11, which uses prayer and meditation to improve your contact with God. Moreover, it helps ground you and enriches your spiritual life, your self-knowledge, and your wisdom.

The famous prayer of St. Ignatius, part of the "contemplation to gain love,"[126] captures the essence of the twelve-step program, especially Steps 3 and 11:

> Take, Lord, and receive
> all my liberty,
> my memory, my understanding and my entire will—
> all that I have and call my own
> You have given it all to me.
> To you, Lord, I return it.
> Everything is yours; do with it what you will.
> Give me only your love and your grace.
> That is enough for me.

Another way of implementing Step 11 in your daily life is to simply place yourself in the presence of God and to ask God to direct your daily life in the way God wants, and in the way that will serve God. In praying for what you want, you specifically ask for interior knowledge of all the good you have received from God.[127] You can leave the results of your prayer up to God. In the ups and downs of everyday life, God alone can bring about consolation without any necessary causes.[128] Grace can touch your life, reassuring you of the relationship you share with God.

When doing the Ignatian Spiritual Exercises recently, while noticing and discerning these interior movements of my heart and inner world that Ignatius asks us to do, I found myself looking through my prayer journal to see what it was that left me feeling consoled or desolated. I often found that minor fears and irritations left me with a feeling of being in limbo, of being powerless or agitated, and those were things I needed to watch out for as precursors to desolation.

I also found that when I was asked to contemplate the Eucharist, specifically the "do this in memory of me" prayer during Mass, I felt a peace of mind and a desire to put that into action. I gave thanks for the peaceful sense of purpose I received, and I gained a greater sense of understanding how "through him we live and move and have our being."

On a recent trip to Bali, Indonesia, I found Hindu spirituality compelling in that it acknowledged both the good and the bad spirits operating in the world. I laughed when I saw people putting out gifts on plates in the street: sweets, lit cigarettes, even alcohol, to appease all the gods! When I asked a local what was going on, he said they were acknowledging and paying homage to both the good and the evil spirits. I liked this, because it was acknowledging that we all operate with these elements within us. There was also an overriding homage to nature, which had a calming effect on me spiritually. It reminded me of Ignatius's advice in the Spiritual Exercises to pay homage to God in creation and to God's gifts in creation. When I contemplated this idea,

I felt a greater sense of being part of an organic whole and appreciating the humanity of all peoples. I found this to be a great gift of light, of illumination, as Ignatius would say.

Crucially, the prayer relationship between you and God is akin to that of lovers. In Ignatian terms, love consists "in the lover's giving and communicating to the beloved what he has or out of what he has."[129] This intimacy, also known as love mysticism, is what you can strive for in Step 11, that is, a genuine relationship of giving and receiving between the beloved and the lover.

The Beguines were a famous group of laywomen in the twelfth century who left a profound example of spiritual devotion. Their movement originated in Belgium and spread throughout Europe during the thirteenth century. The uniqueness of these women came from the way they blurred the boundaries between religious life and life in a lay community; they worked to earn a living while living devout lives. They did not take permanent vows but instead would often move in and out of religious life. Their emphasis was on charity, humility, and companionship.

The role of visions in the life of these women was profoundly illuminative and expressive of the new Eucharistic devotion of the twelfth century, characterised by a reverence for Christ's presence in the Mass and the union between the soul of the person and Christ, and marked by an emphasis on the humanity and passion of Christ. The mysticism of their visions was particularly personal, intimate, humane, and feminine, embodying an empathy with the ordinary person. The Beguines did not shy away from pain or suffering, or from the darkness or absence of God, and they primarily focused on love as the ultimate expression of God.

The Beguine spirituality is extremely complementary to a twelve-step journey, and discussion of it brings to mind an epiphany I had approximately fifteen years ago at a Benedictine monastery not too far from Sydney. I was praying in the chapel in front of the Blessed Sacrament, which Catholics believe is the presence of Christ. I had normally not had much interest in such devotion, but as a relatively new Catholic, I sat in the chapel, not expecting anything and not praying for anything in particular. At some point, I am not sure when, I experienced what I can only describe as a mystical experience. I was shown all of my life as a rich tapestry of many colors. It was as if God was showing me exactly what my life meant and how every piece fit together like a beautiful puzzle. I remember that somehow it all made sense. It is hard to explain, but this experience inspired a state of ecstasy that lasted for hours, and I remember the impression it made on me. What I learned from that experience of great consolation was to go to prayer with an open heart, to try not to expect anything, but to leave my heart open and empty for God to speak to me.

Julian of Norwich's example to the world also lies in her extraordinary compassion, her wisdom dispensed to her local community, her willingness to submit to the will of God, and her incredible appreciation of the role of God's grace, which is essential for those of us fulfilling this step of prayer and meditation. "With all the will of my heart I assented wholly to be as was God's will,"[130] she says, and "Our Lord showed me a spiritual sight of his familiar love. I saw that he is to us everything which is good and comforting for our help."[131]

The aim of Step 11 is not self-depreciation, but emptying yourself for God, living with a broader connection to the world, and putting your relationship with God first. However, not all times of prayer and meditation will leave you feeling connected to God or a higher power. Julian understood our need to be comforted by God in some instances and left to our own devices in others. Regarding those times in the spiritual desert, when you do not necessarily feel any spiritual presence, Julian saw in her vision

that every [person] needs to experience this,
to be comforted at one time,
and at another to fail and to be left to [him- or herself].
God wishes us to know
that he keeps us safe all the time,
in joy and in sorrow, and that he loves
us as much in sorrow as in joy. . . .
Therefore, it is not God's will that when we feel
pain we should pursue it, sorrowing and mourning
for it, but that suddenly we should pass it over and
preserve ourselves in endless delight, because God is
almighty, our lover and preserver.[132]

Sometimes, your difficulties in life may be part of God calling you in mysterious ways, the desire of God for you, the desire of God to be known by you:

[God] wants us to accept our tarrying and our suffering
as lightly as we are able,
and to count them as nothing . . . because of
our love. . . . [T]herefore if a [person] be in so much
pain, so much woe, and so much unrest that
it seems to him that he can think of nothing at
all but the state he is in or what he is feeling,
let him, as soon as he may, pass it over lightly
and count it as nothing. Why? Because God
wants to be known.[133]

To practice prayer and meditation, you also need to remind yourself that without love, you have no spiritual life. The love of God that changes and transforms us is the epitome of the gift of self. God changes people who feel incapable of change. As Paul's famous passage from Corinthians reminds us:

And if I have prophetic powers, and understand all mysteries and all knowledge, and if I have all faith, so as to remove mountains, but do not have love, I am nothing. If I give away all my possessions, and if I hand over my body so that I may boast, but do not have love, I gain nothing. . . . Love never ends. . . . And now faith, hope, and love abide, these three; and the greatest of these is love. (1 Corinthians 13:2–13)

St. Francis of Assisi, a mystic of the early thirteenth century, knew only too well that praying in a state of humility was the pathway to God. One of Francis's most life-changing experiences was meeting and embracing a leper. Another was his call to serve God. His famous prayer embodies the spirit of Step 11 and is an ideal prayer to say at the beginning of your day:

> Most high
> Glorious God,
> Enlighten the darkness of my heart
> And give me, Lord,
> A correct faith,
> A certain hope,
> A perfect charity,
> Sense and knowledge,
> So that I may carry out Your holy
> And true command.
> Amen.

Francis came from a wealthy family, and his meeting with the leper was most probably very difficult for him. He might have felt the immense presence of God in the leper's suffering, the poverty of Christ, or the emptiness and poverty of spirit in another human being. This event led to his conversion. He stripped naked before the local bishop and his father as a symbolic rejection of wealth and an adoption of poverty. It is said that his great experience of the poverty and humility of Christ made him the first recorded case of someone receiving the stigmata.

In summary, your goal in Step 11 is greater intimacy with God, "the raising of the heart and mind to God."[134] It is for God to open your

spiritual eyes and show you your soul in the midst of your heart.[135]
Prayer and meditation give you a sense of belonging and a deep con-
viction that, regardless of what goes on around you, all will be well.
The Pauline letters of Scripture are full of such reassurances: "Now
to him who by the power at work within us is able to accomplish
abundantly far more than all we can ask or imagine, to him be glory"
(Ephesians 3:20–21).

12

Faith without Works Is Dead

Step 12: Having had a spiritual awakening as a result of these Steps, we tried to carry this message to alcoholics and to practice these principles in all our affairs.

I don't think happiness or unhappiness is the point. How do we meet the problems we face? How do we best learn from them and transmit what we have learned to others, if they would receive the knowledge?

In my view, we of this world are pupils in a great school of life. It is intended that we try to grow, and that we try to help our fellow travelers to grow in the kind of love that makes no demands. In short, we try to move toward the image and likeness of God as we understand Him.

When pain comes, we are expected to learn from it willingly, and help others to learn. When happiness comes, we accept it as a gift, and thank God for it.

—Bill W.[136]

Graham's Story

"For me Step 12 has always been about freedom from the bondage of self through helping others. Sure, there is a certain amount of altruism involved, but primarily when I am helping someone else, it takes the focus off me. It gets back to what Socrates said on living the good life. He claimed that wisdom was knowledge, because if everyone knew how good it made them feel and how beneficial it was for them when they helped others, everyone would do it. The biggest single problem confronting most people is egocentrism in varying degrees.

"For me it is like an emotional chain, and every time I do some form of service work it breaks another link in the chain. Anyone can do service work—a kind word when you're not in the mood, a smile at a passing stranger—it is all service work and aids and abets your spiritual well-being. I think the most important gift I can give anyone is my time. Sure, I can give someone food or money, or dispense some pithy wisdom, but to give up your time to someone, that is real service work. Going the extra distance, taking time out when there is nothing in it for me, these are ways I can do 'service' in the workplace and in any other area of my life."

Actions Speak

One source of inspiration for twelve-step programs in their early formation was the philosophy that "faith without works is dead." James's letter in the New Testament talks about this (James 2:18). Step 12 has as its underlying philosophy that if you truly have a spiritual awakening, you need to take your spiritual awareness out into the world and help others (James 1:22–25). Graham's reflection shows that sometimes it is the simple act of being there for others and giving that person your time that constitutes "helping others."

In practicing these principles in all your affairs, remember that there are three powerful forces that can lead you away from the spiritual life: power, prestige, and possession. The goal of a balanced life, of course, is for things like money to become your servant, not your master. Thus, your spiritual condition takes precedence over your material condition. Freedom from fear is far more important than freedom from want.[137]

The twelve-step journey is an awakening of your heart and mind to God, and in Step 12, you can see God around you in other people, as well as the presence of the Spirit, when you help others. As the book *Twelve Steps and Twelve Traditions* points out, no form of external reward could be a substitute for service:

> Service, gladly rendered, obligations squarely met, troubles well accepted or solved with God's help, the knowledge that at home or in the world outside we are partners in a common effort, the well-understood fact that in God's sight all human beings are important, the proof that love freely given surely brings a full return, the certainty that we are no longer isolated and alone in self-constructed prisons, the surety that we need no longer be square pegs in round holes but can fit and belong in God's scheme of things. . . . True ambition is not what we thought it was. True ambition is the desire to live usefully and walk humbly under the grace of God.[138]

An Aboriginal recovering alcoholic I once met said, "Know yourself, be yourself, forgive yourself and others, then forget yourself." This describes well this process of self-knowledge in the twelve steps and of trying to not be so self-centered, to "let go of self" and help others. It is also a process that involves several key elements of the Christian spiritual tradition: a constant striving for detachment and a focus on connection.

In reconnecting with your real self—the "unedited" version of yourself—and with God, you are in a position to go out and help others in whatever way you feel called to do so. It is important that you do this unconditionally, with "a love that makes no demands," as Bill W. said. That way, you know you are truly not out for personal gain or self-centered needs.

Many of the personal stories in this book have shown how such a way of being can lead to enhanced spiritual health and relief from states like depression. Bill W., himself a sufferer from bouts of depression, apparently always recommended long walks and good deeds as a remedy for malaise.

The journey of self-discovery through the twelve steps may have put you more in touch with your own gifts. So you can now use them to enhance your own life and those of others. For example, you may have discovered that you have an artistic bent and now have a great avenue for self-expression. Someone who is struggling may realize that such an avenue can be therapeutic. This is all part of practicing the principles of the twelve steps in all your affairs.

In the Old Testament, the Israelites became lost and disconnected when they forgot their own story, when they forgot the debt they owed to God. So it is with you and with communities. You need to remember what and where you have come from in order to stay on your spiritual path and to enrich your own and other people's lives. So, on this journey you need to connect to your own life story; to understand how it has influenced you as well as what and where you have come from; and to connect to a higher power, which in turn will open you up to connect with others.

The late Thomas Merton, a Trappist monk, is famous for his writing on contemplative prayer. After pursuing a literary career in New York, Merton converted to Catholicism and joined monastic life in the 1940s. Merton saw the difficulty in trying to live a spiritual, contemplative life in a world that focuses on the rational and the competitive, on achievement and a "winning is everything" philosophy. To be in the world but not of it, not dictated by its illusions, but able to partake in it, is a challenge. How can you be open to embrace all of life but still partake in an openness, emptiness, and poverty of spirit, as the mystics did?

Practicing these principles in all your affairs may be as simple as taking your spiritual wisdom and contemplation into your own world of action, and letting others see that there is something powerful within you that sustains you. An example of this might be not allowing yourself to be drawn into petty squabbles in a work situation but instead keeping focused on your own tasks for that day. Having a spiritual awakening as a result of the twelve steps might mean being grateful for the fact that an addiction no longer controls you, or being grateful for the way in which you were led to be free of that addiction.

Thomas Merton also stresses the importance of remaining connected to your own story, of owning your own experience and understanding how all of it has affected your life, and of seeing God's work in the pattern of your life:

> Let us keep alive especially the awareness of what is really authentic within our own experience, because we know, we have experienced in moments of prayer, in moments of truth and realization, what God really asks of us and what God really wishes to give us. Let us remain faithful to that truth and to that experience.[139]

Step 12 is about integrating much of what you have learned along the way in your spiritual journey. After I left behind my "purgation decade," the 2000s, my life has become more about balance. Faith has infiltrated every area of my life in a gentler way, and I think acceptance is part of this. My own longing has taken me outside of myself.

I also believe that my own suffering has caused me to be a more compassionate human being, and this has helped my work. As a hospital chaplain, I carry my years of life experience with me when I enter into a room; my own brokenness and history are threads of wisdom, a gift to bring others. I experience my own "private chapel" of sacred encounter with other people. This is what being a chaplain really is about, and what the word *chaplain* really means.

My intuition has often been my guide. When I listen to my intuition in the quiet moments of prayer or meditation, I know God is speaking my truth. One of my favorite passages of Scripture is Romans 12:2: "Do not be conformed to this world, but be transformed by the renewing of your minds, so that you may discern what is the will of God—what is good and acceptable and perfect."

The mystics offered an excellent example of integrated consciousness as they went about their lives. For example, Mechthild taught that
desire for God is our greatest treasure;[140] Teresa of Ávila, that Jesus or
God is our friend; and Julian of Norwich, that Jesus is also our mother:
"And then will the bliss of our motherhood in Christ be to begin anew
in the joys of our Father, God, which new beginnings will last, newly
beginning without end."[141]

The twelfth-century Benedictine Hildegard of Bingen also put forward a holistic spirituality that was cosmic in scope and unique in its
feminine expression and breadth of comprehension of human nature.
Tithing was not an uncommon practice in medieval Europe, and as
the tenth child of a noble family, Hildegard was placed at an early age
in the care of a recluse, Jutta, who lived in a nearby religious community. Jutta later founded a Benedictine convent, and Hildegard became
a Benedictine nun at the age of eighteen. She had supernatural visions
from a young age, and when she became abbess of the Benedictine
community in 1136, she began recording some of her visionary experiences. Even a commission by the pope of the day, Pope Innocent II,
proclaimed her visions to be of genuine divine inspiration. She was
not only a mystic but also a musician, poet, artist, and what we might
call a naturopath today. She was also a friend and adviser to kings and
queens, as well as monastics, and a woman who sought to reform the
church. Hildegard understood that there was a cosmic force of unity
operating in the universe:

> O most steadfast path,
> Which penetrates all things: in the highest places, on the
>   plains,
> And in every abyss,
> You summon and unite all.[142]

What makes Hildegard unique among her contemporaries in
late-medieval society is that her writings, and in particular her visions,

captured a cosmic, interconnected holistic approach to life while still espousing the Benedictine values of unity, balance, harmony, and stability. This universal, creation-centered view of theology and humankind reflected the cycles of life, valued the feminine, and did not shy from the complementarities of the divine and the human.

Hildegard's writings also reflect the mood of the prevalent Christian Renaissance humanism at that time, in which knowledge and faith were held in high esteem, and spirituality was deeply affected by the personal and the human. Love and the soul's yearning for union with the divine were emphasized, as was the positive nature of the human being.

Described as embodying poverty of spirit, Hildegard always paid homage to the glory of God and stressed that only the humble possess true vision. Her mystical path is that of asceticism and detachment, prayer and contemplation. Following her path allows for periods of spiritual aridity in order to emerge with true humility and a right relationship between self and God. This, and her emphasis on the humanity of Christ, makes her a source of wisdom and inspiration for us today.

I remember one day years ago, when I was racing to get to Mass to receive Holy Communion, knowing that I was too late for the homily or readings but knowing that I needed to receive. This hunger did not involve my intellect; it involved my heart and was not rational. There are desires, thoughts that cannot be manufactured, that are not part of "I should" or "This is the way I'm told it should be." Instead, they come naturally—the graced moments of insight and consolation, as Ignatius would call them, those experiences of mystery that cannot be explained through conditioning or anything else. These things are all part of having a spiritual awakening.

As you try to put Step 12 into practice in your daily life, you need to integrate your spiritual experience and your life experience, both good and bad. To somehow help others and change the society in which you live, you need to carry with you self-knowledge, humility, and charity. Most importantly, you need to remind yourself, as the anonymous fourteenth-century author of *The Cloud of Unknowing* wrote: "It is love alone that can reach God in this life, and not knowing."[143]

Conclusion

My Story: Driving along a New Road

Driving around every curve, with windswept hair and feeling freed by the breeze, the enormous sound of the great southern Indian Ocean greeting me at every turn, I could feel the increased sense of freedom on that car journey in late 2009. I was revisiting those words Jesus told Nicodemus: "You must be born from above" (John 3:7). I was coming around again—a cleansing, a healing, a purgation, was taking place.

I lived like a nomad for the following six months. It was a year before I started to feel settled again. Moving from that point of having felt distant from God, I started to feel well again, my faith slowly came back, and I began to rebuild my life. My road trip became a metaphor for my life, and a wisdom and fearlessness emerged out of it. Now I am reminded of the words of the famous 1960s beat-generation writer Jack Kerouac, of *On the Road* fame: "The only thing I have to offer is my confusion," albeit a rich well of wisdom and blessings in that confusion.

I recently watched a television miniseries called *The Pillars of the Earth*, based on the bestselling novel by Ken Follett, about the building of a cathedral in England centuries ago, something that took many decades and generations of hard work, setbacks, and dramas. The show got me to thinking about how my life is like a cathedral, a constant work in progress.

Each time I move forward, I carry with me my own brokenness and history. Time heals and reveals, and while I have peeled away many layers of the onion, I find myself still at the mercy of the waves of consolation and desolation that flow through my life, yet still able to tune into my overarching spirituality and listen to my intuition.

The graced moments of insight and consolation bring moments of wisdom and joy. Epiphanies like my experience at the abbey in Jamberoo before the Blessed Sacrament or my return to faith are beautiful stepping-stones of my own spiritual journey. As the Jesuit Karl Rahner said, it is the good and beautiful things of life that "promise and point to eternal light and everlasting life."[144] My own life appears to have demonstrated that "the devout Christian of the future will either be a 'mystic,' one who has 'experienced' something, or he [or she] will cease to be anything at all."[145]

So as I go about my journey seeking peace, love, and purpose, trusting my own intuition as I go, I am waiting, continually turning, like the Benedictines; listening to my heart like the monastics; and turning to find God in the light and in the darkness, like so many mystics. Like Ignatius, I look for the illumination in my day and signs of consolation and desolation. As much as the idea of "the emergence of the true self" may sound trite, it still rings true for me. As the Spirit gently breathes on me, I see how grace, from the small mustard seed of faith that began in 1983, has blossomed into the tree of life.

This journey of freedom with the twelve steps and the Christian mystical tradition is an uncertain one that starts with the admission of powerlessness and ultimately brings freedom from bondage. The twelve-step movement—which began when two human beings suffering the same burden helped each other—tapped into great truths about the human condition. Perhaps, as the Swiss psychiatrist Paul

Tournier said when describing the Oxford Group, which played a big part in the early formation of the steps, it may well have also done what the church was failing to do at that time: "[finding] out what was happening in people's souls. . . . There is still too much talking, but silence has returned. Frank [Buchman, the founder of the Oxford Group] helped to show again that the power of silence is the power of God."[146]

As we pass through the twenty-first century, the words of the famous Benedictine monk, Bede Griffiths, who resided in an Indian ashram and died two decades ago, still ring true. He speaks of a reconnection, a force that is transforming humanity. All over the world, despite the existence of much turmoil and suffering, more and more people are turning to a spiritual path, looking to the inner center of the heart and inner reality to find meaning in life.[147] Many are seeking what Karl Rahner described as "the holy mystery," the mystery behind everything.

The path of the twelve steps, like the paths of the great mystics, may involve trying to let go of things that hold you back from God. The spiritual life can sometimes be painful, but it is always mysterious and ultimately fulfilling. As Mechthild of Magdeburg reminds us:

God leads his chosen children
Along strange paths
And it is a strange path
And a noble path,
Which God himself walked.[148]

And in closing, as Bill W. once said, "You are asking yourself, as all of us must: 'Who am I' . . . 'Where am I?' . . . 'Whence do I go?' The process of enlightenment is usually slow. But, in the end, our seeking always brings a finding. These great mysteries are, after all, enshrined in complete simplicity."[149]

Acknowledgments

The Twelve Steps of Alcoholics Anonymous and excerpts from *Daily Reflections*, *The Twelve Steps and Twelve Traditions*, *Alcoholics Anonymous*, and *Came to Believe* are reprinted with the permission of Alcoholics Anonymous World Services (AAWS).

Permission to reprint the Twelve Steps and these excerpts does not mean that AAWS has reviewed or approved the contents of this publication or that AAWS necessarily agrees with the views expressed herein. AA is a program of recovery from alcoholism only—use of the Twelve Steps and these excerpts in connection with programs and activities that are patterned after AA, but that address other problems, or in any other non-AA context, does not imply otherwise. Although Alcoholics Anonymous is a spiritual program, AA is not a religious program, and use of AA material in its present connection does not imply AA's affiliation with or endorsement of, any sect, denomination, or specific religious belief.

Quotes from *The Best of Bill W.*, published by the Grapevine, are reprinted with permission from The AA Grapevine Inc., New York.

I am particularly grateful to Alcoholics Anonymous World Service Office in New York and the *AA Grapevine* for allowing me to liberally use their material. I hope I have given it the respect it deserves.

I would especially like to thank the late Father Brian Stoney for his feedback, love, guidance, and support with the original book, and in spirit with this revised edition, particularly with the references to St. Ignatius. Also, the Loyola Institute at Pymble, New South Wales, Australia, and Father Michael Ryan, SJ, for his spiritual guidance while I completed the Ignatian Spiritual Exercises in daily life. Also Father Michael Smith, SJ, for his retreat on Ignatian discernment in the 1990s. Also, I thank Ed Campion for his encouragement of me as a writer. I would also like to thank the nuns at the Benedictine Abbey in Jamberoo, New South Wales, for their guidance and insight and for providing a place of worship, contemplation, and marvelous epiphanies over the years.

I thank my friend Diane Young for her publishing expertise, wisdom, and discerning eye, as well as the Australian Society of Authors. Also, I thank my scriptwriting teacher, Karel Segers, for his wonderful insights into the theme of the hero's journey in storytelling; my dear friend Bridie Carter, for her emotional and spiritual insight in regard to my work; Dianne Wells, for her moral support; and Carla Todaro, for her insights.

In particular, I thank the Varuna Writers House in Katoomba, New South Wales, for giving me the opportunity to focus and work in the house of the famous Australian writer Eleanor Dark.

Thanks again to those friends and acquaintances who have allowed me to use their stories for this book.

I apologize for all the times I have failed to use inclusive language in this book. Since most of the texts are very old, and many of the twelve-step texts were written in the first half of the twentieth century, it is difficult to maintain consistent attention to inclusiveness. However, I hope that a spirit of inclusiveness comes through.

The author would like to acknowledge the kind permission given by the following sources to reproduce material. Every effort has been made to contact the holders of copyright material. Any mistakes or omissions will be corrected in the next printing of this book.

Alisa Hamilton (Constable and Company Publishers) for *Frank Buchman: A Life*, Great Britain, copyright 1985.

Joy West, wife of Morris West, and the Melaleuca Investment Party Ltd, for Morris West's *A View from the Ridge*. (HarperSan Francisco, 1994).

HarperCollins Publishers, New York and San Francisco, for *The Gospel of Thomas in The Complete Gospels*. Edited by Robert J. Miller. Sonoma, copyright 1992.

Carol Lee Flinders for her book *A Little Book of Women Mystics*, 1995.

Carl Jung, *Memories, Dreams, Reflections*, 1963. Reprinted by permission of HarperCollins Publishers Ltd.

The Regents of the University of California for Barbara Newman's *Sister of Wisdom: St. Hildegard's Theology of the Feminine*. Copyright 1987.

Paulist Press Inc. New York/Mahwah, NJ: *John Cassian Conferences* in CWS series, C. Luibheid Ed., copyright 1985; Origen, *An Exhortation to Martyrdom, Prayer and Selected Works*. Translated by Rowan A. Greer. Copyright 1979.

Permission of The Thomas Merton Legacy Trust, for all mention of Thomas Merton's works.

Darton, Longman and Todd Ltd., London, for *Bede Griffiths' The New Creation in Christ*, copyright 1992.

Liturgical Press for *The Rule of St. Benedict in English*, Philadelphia, copyright 1978.

Bibliography

Agassi, Andre. *Open: An Autobiography*. London: HarperCollins, 2009.

Alcoholics Anonymous. New York: Alcoholics Anonymous World Services, 1976.

Armstrong, Karen. *The Spiral Staircase*. London: HarperPerennial, 2005.

As Bill Sees It. New York: Alcoholics Anonymous World Services, 1967.

Augustine. *Confessions*. Trans. R. S. Pine-Coffin. Middlesex, UK: Penguin, 1961.

———. *Selected Writings*. Trans. Mary T. Clark. New York: Paulist Press, 1984.

Bill W. "Alcoholics Anonymous Beginnings and Growth" (talk presented to the New York City Medical Society on Alcoholism, April 28, 1958). In *Three Talks to Medical Societies by Bill W., Co-Founder of AA*, pp. 8–48. New York: Alcoholics Anonymous World Services.

———. "Basic Concepts of Alcoholics Anonymous" (excerpts from an address presented to the Medical Society of the State of New

York, Section on Neurology and Psychiatry Annual Meeting, New York, May 1944). In *Three Talks to Medical Societies by Bill W., Co-Founder of AA*, pp. 1–48. New York: Alcoholics Anonymous World Services.

————. "This Matter of Fear." In *The Best of Bill: From the Grapevine*. New York: AA Grapevine, 1990. Also in *The Language of the Heart, Bill W.'s Grapevine Writings*, pp. 265–269. New York: AA Grapevine Inc., 1988.

Boulding, Maria, O.S.B. *St. Benedict of Nursia*.

Bowie, Fiona. *Beguine Spirituality: An Anthology*. Trans. Oliver Davies. London: SPCK, 1989.

Brundell, Michael. "Discovering the Diamond, Signposts for the Inner Journey: The Interior Castle of Saint Teresa of Avila." *Spirituality* 2, no. 6 (May–June 1996).

Came to Believe. New York: Alcoholics Anonymous World Services, 1973.

Cameron, Peter John. *The Classics of Catholic Spirituality*. New York: Alba House, 1996.

Capps, W. H., and W. M. Wright, eds. *Silent Fire: An Invitation to Western Mysticism*. New York: HarperCollins, 1978.

Carver, Raymond. *Fires*. London: Vintage, 2009.

Cassian, John. *Conference 10*. The Second Conference of the Abbot Isaac on Prayer. Translation by Colm Luibheid. New York: Paulist Press, 1985.

The Collected Works of John of the Cross. Trans. Kieran Kavanaugh and Otilio Rodriguez. Washington, DC: ICS Publications, 1973.

Costelloe, Morgan. "The Spirituality of Matt Talbot." *Spirituality* (1997): 12. Dublin.

Daily Reflections. New York: Alcoholics Anonymous World
Services, 1990.

Delmage, Lewis, SJ, ed. *The Spiritual Exercises of St. Ignatius Loyola.*
Philadelphia: St. Paul Editions, 1978.

de Vinck, José, ed. *Revelations of Women Mystics from Middle Ages to
Modern Times.* New York: Alba House, 1985.

De Waal, Esther. *Seeking God: The Way of St. Benedict.* London:
Fount, 1996.

Dumm, Demetrius. *Flowers in the Desert.* Mahwah, NJ: Paulist
Press, 1987.

Egan, H. *Karl Rahner: Mystic of Everyday Life.* New York:
Crossroad, 1998.

Farrow, Mia. *What Falls Away.* New York: Bantam, 1997.

Fleming, David L., SJ. *The Spiritual Exercises of St. Ignatius, A Literal
Translation and a Contemporary Reading.* Trans. Elder
Mullen, SJ. St. Louis: Institute of Jesuit Sources, 1978.

———. *What Is Ignatian Spirituality?* Chicago: Loyola Press, 2008.

Flinders, Carol Lee, ed. *A Little Book of Women Mystics.* San
Francisco: HarperSanFrancisco, 1995.

Fox, Matthew. *Illuminations of Hildegard of Bingen.* Santa Fe, NM:
Bear and Co., 1987.

Francis of Assisi. "The Writings." In *Classics of Western Spirituality,*
translation by Regis. J. Armstrong and I. C. Brady. Mahwah,
NJ: Paulist Press International, 1991.

Frankl, Victor. *Man's Search for Meaning.* New York: Washington
Square Press, 1984.

Fry, Timothy, ed. *The Rule of St. Benedict in English.* Collegeville,
MN: Liturgical Press, 1982.

Furlong, Monica. *Visions and Longings*. London: Mowbrays, 1950.

Gilbert, Elizabeth. *Eat, Pray, Love: One Woman's Search for Everything across Italy, India, and Indonesia*. London: Bloomsbury, 2006.

"The Gospel of Thomas." In *The Complete Gospels*, ed. Robert J. Miller, pp. 301–324. Sonoma, CA: HarperSanFrancisco, 1992.

Griffiths, Bede. *The New Creation in Christ*. London: Darton, Longman, & Todd, 1992.

Hansen, Michael, SJ. "Progress in Divine Love," Book of Desires. St. Ignatius 4 Week Retreat in Daily Life.

Happold, F. C., ed. *Mysticism: A Study and an Anthology*. London: Pelican, 1970.

Hicks, David. *Guantanamo: My Journey*. North Sydney: Random House Australia, 2010.

Hildegard of Bingen. *Book of Divine Works I*. Ed. Matthew Fox. Santa Fe, NM: Bear & Co., 1987.

"Scivias." In *Hildegard of Bingen: An Anthology*, ed. F. Bowie and O. Davies. London: SPCK, 1990.

Jager, Willigis. *Search for the Meaning of Life: Essays and Reflections on the Mystical Experience*. St. Louis: Triumph, 1995.

John Cassian Conferences. Ed. C. Luibheid. CWS Series. New York, 1985.

Joyce, James. *A Portrait of the Artist as a Young Man*. Bath, UK: Chivers, 1978.

Jung, Carl. *Memories, Dreams, Reflections*. Ed. Aniela Jaffe. London: Collins, 1963.

Kerouac, Jack. *On the Road*. 1957. London: Penguin.

Lean, Garth. *Frank Buchman: A Life*. London: Constable and Co., 1985.

The Lives of the Desert Fathers. Intro. Benedicta Ward. Trans. Norman Russell. Collegeville, MN: Cistercian Publications, 1980.

Main, John. *Christian Meditation: The Gethsemani Talks.* Benedictine Priory of Montreal: Christian Meditation Media, 1982.

————. *Christian Mysteries: Prayer and Sacrament.* Montreal: Benedictine Priory of Montreal, 1979.

Matthew, Iain. *The Impact of God.* London: Hodder & Stoughton, 1995.

May, Gerald. *Addiction and Grace.* New York: Harper One, 2007.

McGinn, Bernard, John Meyendorff, and Jean Leclercq, eds. *Christian Spirituality.* New York: Crossroad, 1985.

Merton, Thomas. *Contemplation in a World of Action.* London: Unwin Paperbacks, 1980.

New Jerusalem Bible. London: Darton, Longman & Todd, 1985.

Newman, Barbara. *Sister of Wisdom: St. Hildegard's Theology of the Feminine.* Los Angeles: University of California Press, 1987.

Origen. *An Exhortation to Martyrdom, Prayer & Selected Works.* Trans. Rowan A. Greer. New York: Paulist Press, 1979.

Rahner, Karl, SJ. *Christian Living Formerly and Today.* Trans. David Bourke. Theological Investigations No. 7. New York: Seabury.

————. "Experiencing the Spirit." In *The Practice of Faith: A Handbook of Contemporary Spirituality*, ed. Karl Lehmann and Albert Raffelt. New York: Crossroad Publishing, 1983.

————. *Mission and Grace.* London: Sheed and Ward, 1966.

Rohr, Richard. *Male Spirituality* (tape). Sydney: Aquinas Academy, 2000.

Simmons, Henry C. *In the Footsteps of the Mystics.* Mahwah, NJ: Paulist Press, 1992.

Tarnas, Richard. *The Passion of the Western Mind*. London: Pimlico, 1991.

Thomsen, Robert. *Bill W*. London: Hamish Hamilton, 1975.

Tillich, Paul. *Systematic Theology*. Vol. 3. Chicago: University of Chicago Press, 1963.

Twelve Steps and Twelve Traditions. New York: Alcoholics Anonymous World Services, 1952.

Ward, Benedicta. *The Sayings of the Desert Fathers*. Trans. Benedicta Ward. London: Mowbrays, 1975.

West, Morris. *A View from the Ridge: The Testimony of a Pilgrim*. San Francisco: HarperSanFrancisco, 1994.

Endnotes

1. Baba Kuhi of Shiraz, "The Vision of God in Everything," in *Mysticism: A Study and an Anthology*, by F. C. Happold (London: Pelican Books, 1970), 251.

2. Bede Griffiths, *The New Creation in Christ* (London: Darton, Longman and Todd, 1992), 76.

3. Garth Lean, *Frank Buchman: A Life* (London: Constable and Co., 1985), 31.

4. *Pass It On: The Story of Bill Wilson and How the AA Message Reached the World* (New York: Alcoholics Anonymous World Services, 1984), 127.

5. Bill W., "Alcoholics Anonymous Beginnings and Growth" (talk presented to the New York City Medical Society on Alcoholism, April 28, 1958), in *Three Talks to Medical Societies by Bill W., Co-Founder of AA* (New York: Alcoholics Anonymous World Services), 10.

6. Ibid., 12.

7. "This Matter of Fear" in *The Language of the Heart, Bill W.'s Grapevine Writings* (New York: AA Grapevine Inc., 2011), 15.

8. Ibid., 16.

9. *Alcoholics Anonymous: The Big Book*, 3rd. ed. (New York: Alcoholics Anonymous World Services, 1976), 59–60.

10. Ibid., 17.

11. Carl Jung, *Memories, Dreams, Reflections*, ed. Aniela Jaffe (London: Collins, 1963), 17.

12. Carl Jung, qtd. in Robert Thomsen, *Bill W.* (London: Hamish Hamilton, 1976), 363.

13. Demetrius Dumm, *Flowers in the Desert* (Mahwah, NJ: Paulist Press, 1987), 106.

14. For further explanation of what constitutes a mystic, see F. C. Happold, *Mysticism: A Study and an Anthology* (London: Penguin, 1970), esp. 35–37, 45–47.

15. *Alcoholics Anonymous*, 3rd ed., 60.

16. Bill W., "Alcoholics Anonymous Beginnings and Growth" (talk presented to the New York City Medical Society on Alcoholism, April 28, 1958), in *Three Talks to Medical Societies by Bill W., Co-Founder of AA* (New York: Alcoholics Anonymous World Services), 14.

17. Morgan Costelloe, "The Spirituality of Matt Talbot," in *Spirituality* 12 (1997):178.

18. Dumm, *Flowers in the Desert*, 5.

19. See Paul Tillich's ideas on "new being as process," in *Systematic Theology* 3 (Chicago: University of Chicago Press, 1973): 53.

20. *Alcoholics Anonymous*, 3rd ed. (New York: Alcoholics Anonymous World Services, 1976), 60.

21. Victor Frankl, *Man's Search for Meaning* (New York: Washington Square Press, 1984), 121.

22. Ibid., 5.

23. Dumm, *Flowers in the Desert*, 6.

24. Origen, *First Homily on the Song of Songs*, trans. R. P. Lawson, Ancient Christian Writers 26 (New York: Newman, 1957), 491.

25. Origen, "Homily XXVII on Numbers, bk. 4," in *An Exhortation to Martyrdom, Prayer and Selected Works*, trans. Rowan A. Greer (New York: Paulist Press, 1979), 250–51.

26. John of the Cross, "The Dark Night," in *The Collected Works of John of the Cross*, trans. Kieran Kavanaugh and Otilio Rodriguez (Washington, DC: ICS Publications, 1973), 295.

27. John of the Cross, "The Ascent of Mount Carmel," in *The Collected Works of John of the Cross*, trans. Kavanaugh and Rodriguez, bk. 1, chap. 1–2, no. 13, pp. 74–75, 101–4.

28. See Iain Matthew, *The Impact of God* (London: Hodder and Stoughton, 1995), 26.

29. John of the Cross, "Ascent of Mount Carmel," bk. 2, chap. 4, no. 5, p. 114.

30. John of the Cross, letter 33 (to a Carmelite nun, late 1591), in Matthew, *Impact of God*, 131.

31. Bill W., "Alcoholics Anonymous Beginnings and Growth," 14.

32. "This Matter of Fear," in *The Language of the Heart, Bill W.'s Grapevine Writings* (New York: AA Grapevine Inc., 2011), 267.

33. *Alcoholics Anonymous*, 3rd ed., 60.

34. Morris West, "Lazarus," in *A View from the Ridge* (San Francisco: HarperSanFrancisco, 1994), 135.

35. Qtd. in Robert Thomsen, *Bill W.* (London: Hamish Hamilton, 1975), 363.

36. Carl Jung, *Memories, Dreams, Reflections*, 373.

37. Joseph A. Fitzmeyer, "Pauline Theology," in *The New Jerome Biblical Commentary* (New York: Geoffrey Chapman, 1990), chap. 82, no. 78, p. 1401.

38. J. Behm, "Metamorphoo," in *Theological Dictionary of the New Testament*, eds. Gerhard Kittel, Gerhard Friedrick, Geoffrey William Bromiley (Grand Rapids, MI: Eerdmans, 1985), Vol. 4, p. 757.

39. "St. Ignatius's Prayer," in *The Spiritual Exercises of St. Ignatius: A Literal Translation and a Contemporary Reading*, David L. Fleming, SJ, trans. Elder Mullen, SJ (St. Louis: Institute of Jesuit Sources, 1978), p. 177.

40. *Twelve Steps and Twelve Traditions* (New York: Alcoholics Anonymous World Services, 1978), 36.

41. *Alcoholics Anonymous*, 63.

42. Qtd. in Benedicta Ward, *The Sayings of the Desert Fathers* (Collegeville, MN: Cistercian Publications, 1980), 6–7.

43. Rufinus's prologue to *Historia Monachorum in Aegypto*, in *The Lives of the Desert Fathers*, introduction by Benedicta Ward, trans. Norman Russell (Collegeville, MN: Cistercian Publications, 1980), 50.

44. *Alcoholics Anonymous*, 164.

45. Prologue to *The Rule of St. Benedict in English*, 9–10, ed. Timothy Fry (Collegeville, MN: Liturgical Press, 1982), verses 9–10, p. 15–16.

46. *Alcoholics Anonymous*, 58.

47. In *The Complete Gospels*, ed. Robert J. Miller (Sonoma, CA: HarperSanFrancisco, 1992), 316.

48. *Alcoholics Anonymous*, 71.

49. *Alcoholics Anonymous*, 68.

50. *The Spiritual Exercises of St. Ignatius Loyola*, trans. Lewis Delmage (Boston: St. Paul Editions, 1978), no. 4.

51. Ibid., no. 1.

52. Ibid., no. 43.

53. Ibid., no. 44.

54. Ibid., nos. 316–17.

55. Ibid., no. 6.

56. Ibid., no. 319.

57. Ibid., no. 186.

58. John of the Cross, "The Ascent of Mt. Carmel," bk. 1, chap. 13, stanza 11, p. 104.

59. *John Cassian Conferences*, ed. C. Luibheid, CWS series (New York, 1985), conference 9, chap. 2.

60. Qtd. in Iain Matthew, *The Impact of God*, 24–25.

61. *Twelve Steps and Twelve Traditions*, 125.

62. In *The Complete Gospels*, ed. Miller, 305.

63. *Daily Reflections* (New York: Alcoholics Anonymous World Services, 1990), 107.

64. See John of the Cross's "Ascent of Mt. Carmel," bk 2, ch. 17, verse 3; "Canticle," stanza 23, verse 6; and "The Living Flame of Love," stanza 3 verse 59; qtd. in Matthew, *Impact of God*, 15.

65. *Alcoholics Anonymous*, 68.

66. *The Spiritual Exercises of St. Ignatius: A Literal Translation and a Contemporary Reading*, Fleming, nos. 53–54.

67. *Alcoholics Anonymous*, 69.

68. *The Spiritual Exercises of St. Ignatius*, no. 176.

69. Ibid., no. 135.

70. Ibid., no. 135.

71. Ibid., nos. 136–46.

72. Ibid., no. 327.

73. *John Cassian Conferences*, ed. Luibheid, conference 9, no. 15.

74. Ibid., conference 9, no. 27.

75. *Twelve Steps and Twelve Traditions*, 59.

76. Ibid., 58.

77. John of Lycopolis, qtd. in *The Lives of the Desert Fathers*, trans. Russell, 33.

78. Prologue to *The Rule of St. Benedict in English*, ed. Fry, verse 1, p. 15.

79. Dom John Main, *Christian Mysteries: Prayer and Sacrament* (Montreal: Benedictine Priory of Montreal, 1979), 50.

80. From "Three Sermons on the Song of Songs," trans. A. L. Peck, in F. C. Happold's *Mysticism: A Study and an Anthology* (London: Pelican Books, 1970), 237–38.

81. Julian of Norwich, "Showings," in *Women Mystics*, by Carol Lee Flinders (San Francisco: HarperSanFrancisco, 1995), stanza 258, p. 47.

82. *The Rule of Benedict*, ed. Fry, Chap. 20, verse 3, p. 48.

83. *As Bill Sees It* (New York: Alcoholics Anonymous World Services, 1967), 115.

84. See "Guidelines for the Discernment of Spirits," in *The Spiritual Exercises of St. Ignatius: A Literal Translation and a Contemporary Reading*, Fleming, nos. 314–18.

85. For a contemporary reading of nos. 313–36, see ibid.

86. Ibid., no. 315.

87. Ibid., no. 195.

88. St. Augustine, *Confessions*, trans. R. S. Pine Coffin (Middlesex, UK: Penguin, 1961), bk. 8, ch. 7, p. 169.

89. *Twelve Steps and Twelve Traditions*, 75.

90. *Alcoholics Anonymous*, 76.

91. "Conferences X," in *Christian Meditation: The Gethsemani Talks*, by John Main (Toronto: Christian Meditation Media, 1982), 19.

92. On "three types of people," see *The Spiritual Exercises of St. Ignatius*, nos. 152–55.

93. St. Augustine, *Confessions*, trans. Coffin, bk. 3, ch. 9 p. 67.

94. Ibid., bk. 6, p. 111.

95. Ibid., bk. 8, p. 175.

96. Ibid., bk. 8, ch 12, p. 177.

97. Ibid., bk. 10, p. 231.

98. Ibid., bk. 10, p. 238.

99. Ibid., bk. 8, p. 176.

100. *Alcoholics Anonymous*, 83.

101. *The Spiritual Exercises of St. Ignatius: A Literal Translation and a Contemporary Reading*, Fleming, nos. 189, 198–99, 232–33, 332–33.

102. Prologue to *The Rule of Benedict*, ed. Fry, 35.

103. *The Spiritual Exercises of St. Ignatius: A Literal Translation and a Contemporary Reading*, Fleming, nos. 24–47.

104. Ibid., nos. 189 and 240.

105. Ibid., no. 82.

106. John Main, *The Christian Mysteries: Prayer and Sacrament* (Montreal: Benedictine Priory of Montreal, 1979), 50.

107. Ibid., 47.

108. Richard Rohr, presentation at the seminar "Male Spirituality," Aquinas Academy, Sydney, November 2000.

109. Main, *Christian Mysteries*, 51.

110. Abba Pachomius, in *The Lives of the Desert Fathers*, trans. Russell, 45.

111. Prologue to *The Rule of St. Benedict in English*, verses 35–38, p. 18.

112. Bill W., "Letter, 1964," in *As Bill Sees It* (New York: Alcoholics Anonymous World Services, 1967), 168.

113. *Alcoholics Anonymous*, 84.

114. *Twelve Steps and Twelve Traditions*, 95.

115. *The Spiritual Exercises of St. Ignatius: A Literal Translation and a Contemporary Reading*, Fleming, nos. 314, 315, 317–21.

116. Ibid., no. 322.

117. Ibid., nos. 324, 326–27.

118. Main, *Christian Mysteries: Prayer and Sacrament*, 47.

119. Julian of Norwich, "Showings," in *Visions and Longings* by Monica Furlong (London: Mowbrays, 1950), 191.

120. Ibid., 241.

121. Julian of Norwich, "Showings," in *Revelations of Divine Love* (New York: Penguin Books, 1999), chap. 27, p. 35.

122. Julian of Norwich, "Showings," in Furlong, *Visions and Longings*, 213.

123. Mechthild of Magdeburg, bk VII, verse 56, in *Revelations of Women Mystics from Middle Ages to Modern Times*, ed. José de Vinck (New York: Alba House, 1985), 5–7, 12–23.

124. Teresa of Ávila, "The Interior Castle" in *A Little Book of Women Mystics*, ed. Carol Lee Flinders (San Francisco: HarperSanFrancisco, 1995), 88.

125. Thanks to the nuns at the Benedictine Abbey, Jamberoo, New South Wales, for their weekend lectures on *lectio divina*.

126. *The Spiritual Exercises of St. Ignatius: A Literal Translation and a Contemporary Reading*, Fleming, p. 177.

127. Ibid., no. 233.

128. Ibid., no. 330.

129. Ibid., no. 231.

130. Julian of Norwich, "Showings," in Furlong, *Visions and Longings*, 192.

131. Ibid., 194.

132. Ibid., 204–5.

133. Ibid., 225–26.

134. *Twelve Steps and Twelve Traditions*, 102.

135. Julian of Norwich, "Showings," in Furlong, *Visions and Longings*, 228.

136. Bill W., "Letter, 1950," in *As Bill Sees It*, 306.

137. *Twelve Steps and Twelve Traditions*, 122.

138. Ibid., 124–25.

139. Thomas Merton, *Contemplation in a World of Action* (London: Allen and Unwin, 1980), 355. (Used with permission from the Thomas Merton Legacy Trust.)

140. See her dialogue between the Soul and God in "The Love Chase," in *Revelations of Women Mystics from Middle Ages to Modern Times*, ed. de Vinck, 5–7, 12–23.

141. Julian of Norwich, "Showings," in Furlong, *Visions and Longings*, 246 (see also 236, 238).

142. Hildegard of Bingen, "De Spiritu Sancto" ("To the Holy Spirit"), in *Book of Divine Works*, ed. Matthew Fox (Santa Fe, NM: Bear and Co., 1987), 373.

143. "The Cloud of Unknowing," in *In the Footsteps of the Mystics*, ed. Henry C. Simmons (Mahwah, NJ: Paulist Press, 1992), 138–39.

144. Karl Rahner, "Experiencing the Spirit," in *The Practice of Faith: A Handbook of Contemporary Spirituality*, ed. Karl Lehmann and Albert Raffelt (New York: Crossroad Publishing, 1983), 81, qtd. in H. Egan, *Karl Rahner: Mystic of Everyday Life* (New York: Crossroad Publishing, 1998), 61.

145. Karl Rahner, "Christian Living Formerly and Today," *Theological Investigations*, trans. David Bourke, (New York: Seabury), ch 7, p. 15.

146. Garth Lean, *Frank Buchman: A Life* (London: Constable and Co., 1985), 153.

147. Bede Griffiths, *The New Creation in Christ*, 71.

148. Mechthild of Magdeburg, "On the Way of Suffering for God Joyfully," in Furlong, *Visions and Longings*, 114.

149. Bill W., "Letter, 1955," in *Came to Believe* (New York: Alcoholics Anonymous World Services, 1973), 53.

About the Author

As well as being a published author, Joanna Thyer currently works as a part-time hospital chaplain, and is also an associate university lecturer to medical students, teaching communication skills. Over the years she has also worked in general workplace counseling and chaplaincy, as a drug and alcohol counselor, and as a relationship educator. She holds two university degrees in psychology and theology, has written a screenplay and studied screenwriting, and has a deep interest in the spiritual self-help movement and how it links in with creativity and the search for a meaningful life.